THE LIBRARY OF NATIVE PEOPLES

Warriors *of the* Plains

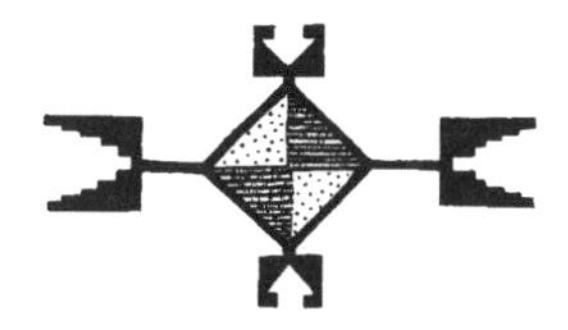

Thomas E. Mails

Illustrations by the Author

COUNCIL OAK BOOKS

Quotes are taken from the following books:

Densmore, Frances. *Teton Sioux Music.* Smithsonian Institution Bureau of American Ethnology, Bulletin 61, 1918.

Dodge, Colonel Richard Irving. *33 Years Among Our Wild Indians.* Archer House, Inc., New York, 1959.

Drannan, Captain William F. *Thirty-one Years on the Plains and in the Mountains.* Thos. W. Jackson Publishing Co., Chicago, 1900.

Grinnell, George Bird. *Blackfoot Lodge Tales and the Story of a Prairie People.* University of Nebraska Press, Lincoln, 1962.

Grinnell, George Bird. *The Story of the Indian.* D. Appleton and Co., New York, 1906.

_______. *When Buffalo Ran.* Yale University Press, New Haven; Humphrey Milford, Oxford University Press, London, 1923.

Kennedy, Michael S. *The Assiniboines.* University of Oklahoma Press, Norman, 1961.

Linderman, Frank B. *Plenty Coups, Chief of the Crows.* University of Nebraska Press, Lincoln, 1962.

Lowie, Robert H. *Indians of the Plains.* Natural History Press, Garden City, New York, 1963.

Mayhall, Mildred P. *The Kiowas.* University of Oklahoma Press, Norman, 1962.

Schultz, James Willard. *My Life as an Indian.* Houghton-Mifflin Co., Boston and New York; Riverside Press, Cambridge, 1906, 1967.

Council Oak Books, Tulsa, OK 74120

Originally published in a slightly different version in
Mystic Warrotrs of the Plains. Copyright © 1972 by Thomas E. Mails.

01 00 99 98 97 5 4 3 2 1

Library of Congress cataloging-in-publication data

Mails, Thomas E.
Warriors of the Plains / Thomas E. Mails; illustrations by the author.
p. cm. — (The Library of Native Peoples)
"Originally published in a slightly different version in Mystic Warriors of the Plains. c1972, c1991"—CIP galley.
ISBN 1-57178-045-9 (alk. paper)
1. Indians of North America—Warfare—Great Plains. I. Mails, Thomas E. Mystic Warriors of the Plains. II. Title. III. Series.
E78.G73M347 1997
978'.00497—dc21 97-12696
CIP

Edited and Designed by Tony Meisel, AM Publishing Services
Printed in the United States of America
ISBN 1-57178-045-9

Contents

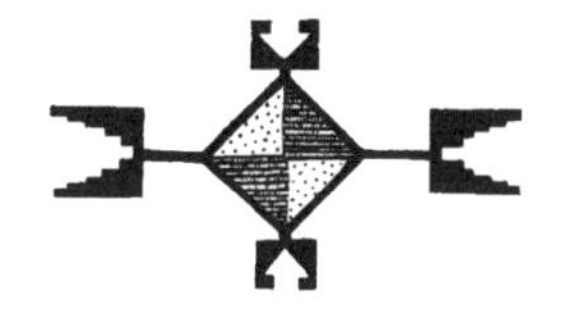

Top, Sioux beaded turtle and sand lizard. *Bottom*, Kiowa woman with child in cradleboard.

The Birth and Training Of the Boy

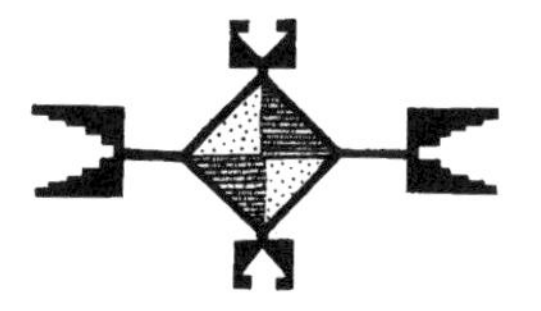

Preparations for the survival and longevity of all Plains warriors began before they were born. During pregnancy, either the mother or one of the grandmothers made two curious quilled or beaded objects, a sand lizard and a turtle. These were gracefully shaped, and finished with horsehair or breath feathers attached to the ends of the four legs. Both animals were revered because they "lived forever" and were so difficult to kill. Their protective power was enlisted early as a guardian and guarantee of the individual's long life. When the child was born, the umbilical cord was cut and placed inside the turtle, packed in tobacco or herbs, while the lizard served as a decoy to lure away malevolent forces. A second use of the turtle was to remind the bearer that his life was a precious gift from his parents, and he had the responsibility to marry and to pass the gift of birth and life on to his own children. Such vigilant protection of life was essential to the Native American's sense of well-being in a land of extremes and unknowns. Obviously, the first step toward survival was to turn one's mind in the direction of whatever was necessary to achieve it.

When the child began to walk, the amulet was attached to his clothing to serve as a constant reminder of its purpose. Therefore, a child of five or six was known as a "carry your navel." Sometimes the turtle was put away later on and other times it was kept by the mother. A boy often tied it to the left shoulder of his shirt, and then transferred it to his buffalo-horned headdress if he became a renowned warrior.

It was the duty of one of the father's sisters to make the cradleboard, and the same loving care as was devoted to the turtle was expended upon it, for it was to be a tangible symbol of sisterly respect, and it maintained the vital bond among the members of the family. After the boy grew, the sight of his beautiful cradle became a continual reminder of this. Even the nature of the cradleboard design contributed to the idea. For example, the Kiowas mounted their cradles on two long boards, with the upper ends sharply pointed so as to stick in the ground and thus protect the baby in case of a head-first fall from a horse.

To avoid the problems of overpopulation in a nomadic society, the Native American family was kept small, consisting usually of one to three children being born from three to five years apart—in any case a second not being encouraged until the first could walk.

If difficulties occurred during labor, and a priest had to be called for a medicine rite before a child was born, the child's turtle was decorated with a small design representing a tortoise, which charmed further dangers away. Thus the tortoise revealed an intimate fact about the person's birth, and it became the first of many marks a man would wear to tell the story of his life.

An ancestral name was given to a child at a festive naming rite a few days after birth, and he kept it until a new name was conferred at a special ceremony honoring his first great accomplishment in life.

Nez Percé boy dressed for festival purposes, wearing otter skin dance chest cover, beaded gauntlets, and roach.

Where other children had already received the prized family names, the father, or else a great warrior of the tribe invited to perform the naming, named the baby according to a war deed the name-bestower had accomplished. He might also name him after a brave animal or something seen in a dream. While a crier, or village herald, reported the name to the entire camp, a wealthy father, following custom, announced that a horse would be given to a specified poor man. Sometimes it would go to another rich man who could return the favor, but this was considered a bit obvious. At this juncture the friends of the family expressed their wish that the child "might live to have his ears pierced," whereupon the father or grandfather announced through the crier that a certain warrior of note would perform the operation. At this time the tribe vowed to protect the child "until it walked." The ear piercing, which was done with a sharp stick and was very painful, took place during the first Sun Dance to be held after the child was able to walk, and the boy wore earrings from then until he died. In the mind of the Native American, ear piercing played, in fact, a role very similar to Jewish circumcision and Christian baptism.

In evidence of the high regard and love in which some Native American children were held, the Sioux had a wonderful ceremony dating from around A.D. 1800 called the Alo' wanpi, or Hunka. The word "Alo' wanpi" meant "to sing for someone," and "Hunka" was the name applied to children participating in the ceremony. A tribesman of renown was invited by the child's father to perform the rite, and the man who performed it was regarded as a second father by the child involved. He made a solemn vow taking the child under his protection until one or the other had died. And he became like a brother to the man whose child or children he sang over and painted with the Hunka ceremonial stripes. In all the great ceremonies of the Sioux there was not one which bound two men together so strongly as this. The tie was even stronger than natural brotherhood, because the invited man had assumed a responsibility not placed on him by nature.

The Alo'wanpi ceremony was a miniature version of the Sun Dance, but without the torture aspects. A special pipe, an altar, a small tree, and a buffalo skull were used, and the ceremonial articles included an ear of corn, a tuft of white down for the child's hair, and a bunch of shed buffalo hair. The pipe was decorated with woodpecker feathers, for this was a simple, humble bird which stayed by its nest and was seldom seen. The bird was considered appropriate because the Hunka child would be more closely guarded and protected than others, and the girls so consecrated were seldom seen in public until they had grown up. The corn was used because of a Sioux legend about the growth of a beautiful plant—which turned out to be corn. The celebration of this ceremony placed a child in a highly respected position in the tribe. Such a child was regarded as possessing that which would make it nothing but good in every way, and was recognized by all as ranking above an ordinary child. (Densmore, *Teton Sioux Music,* pp. 68-77)

The care and responsibility of the infant fell to the mother. She was assisted in this by the grandmother, various sisters and female cousins, or an older daughter. An older sister might care in every way for a girl, but she was limited by custom to feeding and baby-sitting a boy.

Boys ran naked a good part of the time, "since children became tired of their clothes and took them off for relief." Apparel was first required around the age of seven, and the degree of nakedness from then

The boy in training. *a,* catching butterflies for agility. *b,* throwing lance for skill. *c* and *d,* swimming, running for endurance. *e,* Sioux youth carrying special water bag stick used by young man on first war raid.

on depended somewhat upon the sex of the older children in the family.

The disciplining of small children was almost non-existent. In fact, they were catered to and greatly indulged. Children were not permitted to cry, however, and to prevent it their earliest wants were either immediately satisfied, or they were rocked and cuddled until their desires ceased. Where coddling was ineffectual, the grandmother cried along with the child to "help it." The exception among some tribes was that the noses of older children who continued to cry were held, or else water was poured into their nostrils, until the treatment became so intolerable they quit. After all, a group hiding from its enemies in those days could easily be given away by a crying child. Otherwise, children were "asked," not "told," what to do. Ponderous but entertaining lectures about responsibilities began at an early age, and the children had responded so well by the time they were ten or eleven that admonitions about discipline were no longer necessary.

The use of culture frighteners such as the owl, the medicine man, and (later) the White man were sometimes employed to gain obedience from unruly older boys. Children who could not overcome bed-wetting were threatened by being told they would be fed mice, and the Native Americans claim it was an effective remedy.

Native American parents and grandparents openly expressed a great love and fondness for their children, and all Native Americans agree that youngsters were never whipped or handled roughly. Even grown boys who misbehaved were reasoned with until they were able to realize their mistakes.

Native American leaders did recognize that children must be taught, however, "or they will not know anything; if they do not know anything, they will have no sense; and if they have no sense they will not know how to act." (Grinnell, *Blackfoot Lodge Tales,* p. 188) So boys were painstakingly instructed in every matter necessary to a fruitful life.

Parents encouraged the qualities of spirituality, pride, respect for elders, conformance to the tribal code of ethics and to the standard rules of etiquette. Every mother sang instructive lullabys which included lessons in morals and bravery. Tribal historians taught history, and other elders gave instructions in national loyalty.

The father-son relationship took on a special warmth when the father presented his son of four years or so with his first bow and arrows, and began instructing him in shooting, hunting, and trailing techniques. Sometimes uncles or older brothers aided in a boy's development.

By the time they were four or five, children had been given their own clothing, utensils for eating, tools for use in their activities, and a separate bed. They had also received fine garments for participating in festivals. They were expected to take care of these and to keep them in order. Careful attention was paid to the selection of playmates, to dress, and to manners, for children were expected to show the reserve and bearing that elevated family pride. Older children who lacked the qualities of neatness, deportment, respect, and self-control were publicly shamed, since scorn served as a social conditioner for every family.

Children's games were educational, and as such played a significant role in their development. Play between girls and boys was common, and received strong encouragement by the parents. Parents made little tipis, travois, and weapons with which the children could imitate the activities of their elders. The entire play scheme became, in fact, the

Boy tending horse herd.

basic pathway over which the child made a smooth adjustment to adulthood. It continued until the age of eleven years or so, when a strict separation of the sexes was begun, and a more mature training was introduced.

Speed was a secondary aim in their games. Skill, endurance, daring, and the ability to withstand pain were placed at the top of the list, for each of these developed the qualities necessary for national survival. Therefore, the method of choosing leaders in the games was identical to the method of selecting the ranking men for adult activities. They were chosen in accordance with their demonstrated abilities and their successes in contests.

A young boy's first hunting parties were mimic and communal, although without formal organization. Male children less than ten years of age went rabbit hunting together, and also took other small game such as birds and turtles. This was a gratifying and valuable service, for it furnished the family with a supplementary food supply. At the same time, important hunting techniques were being learned. Each son would employ the methods taught him by his father, observe the tricks and approaches used by other boys, and do some experimenting on his own. Above all, they learned to kill for need, rather than for sport or exhibition. On these hunts, young boys learned the first essentials for becoming good providers, cooperative hunters and skillful trackers, and they also learned the laws of survival.

Screech owls, coyotes, wolves, and birds were common to all parts of the Plains, and boys learned to imitate such special animal and bird calls as were chosen by their tribe to be used for communication with each other while hunting, raiding, or fighting.

Boys ten or more years of age were compelled to take long runs, to go without food and water for long periods of time, to roll in the snow, to dive into icy water, and to stay awake and alert for hours on end. As they grew older they took their runs at noon, when the sun was boiling hot. Later still, they were given sacred sweat baths and made to purify themselves in preparation for war. They learned how to throw the lance, and to dodge arrows by spinning or dropping down, to take advantage of any cover, to shoot rapidly from a crouched position, to be able to ride with only their knees guiding the horse, and to swing the shield so as to give the least possible target to an enemy. Among the Sioux, the eyes of the young men were always fixed on the tribe's sacred water bag stick which would be carried by them when they were invited to go on their first raiding party.

The aspiring warrior was trained never to show cowardice, and any such indication gave him a name others never let him forget. No coward ever became a warrior or leader. So young men were placed in situations which would test their courage and alertness to the limit. Once in a "rare" while there was a failure, a boy who didn't have the stuff in him for war and hunting. For him there was no middle ground; he had to put on women's clothing and live his life as a woman. He was not, however, totally scorned, and now and then one of the failures would become the finest craftsman in his village.

Assiniboine elders advised boys to travel on foot as much as possible. "If," they said, "you wish to keep on being a fast runner, you should not ride horses, as your legs will be bowed and your joints will grow fast together." (Kennedy, *The Assiniboines,* p. 36) One of the very first lessons a Crow boy experienced was running to catch butterflies. When onewas caught, its wings were rubbed on the boy's chest to "borrow" the creature's grace, cunning, and swiftness. Other general advice among the Assiniboines went as follows: "Among our people everyone is expected to marry and raise children. In order to make a success of marriage the father must be a good provider—and that means a good hunter. Look to your equipment and use it skillfully. Study the habits of animals and birds and learn to take them at the right time and in the correct manner. Make your kills neatly and quickly, or else you and your family will have to eat sour meat from exhausted game." (Kennedy, p. 39)

The moment a son was big enough to straddle a horse, his father gave him a colt and some gear. He was carefully instructed in the colt's care and was responsible for its well-being thereafter. As boys grew older, they were assigned the responsibility of caring for their parents' herds. The task was usually done by two or more boys at a time, and it gave them an opportunity to ride to their heart's content. It was also a good

Uncle taking nephew on hunting trip.

way to observe the horses' manners and abilities. Often a boy came to know more about what a certain horse could accomplish than his father did.

The young brave had to learn how to get the most out of a horse, and some of the old warriors said that after a White man had completely exhausted one, a Native American could ride the same animal another twenty miles or more. The boy learned how to ride hour upon hour at the fastest possible speed. He was taught that as one horse grew tired and almost fell, he could leap from the back of that one to the back of another while they were both at full gallop. He must even learn to sleep while riding. Groups would divide into sections while being pursued, one section sleeping hanging over their horses' necks, while the other led them—and drove a stolen herd at the same time. Then when all of the horses were exhausted he still must have enough strength left to run on foot! The training was most demanding, and they had plenty of accidents when they were young, although they insisted "they were always happy," and one can readily see why!

Among the Blackfoot, eminent men would make long speeches to groups of boys, telling them what they ought to do to be successful in life. They would point out that to accomplish anything they must be brave and untiring in war; that long life (beyond sixty) was usually not desirable, that old people always had a hard time. The aged were given the worst side of the lodge and generally neglected. It was much better, while the body was strong and in its prime, while the sight was clear, the teeth sound, and the hair still black and long, to die in battle fighting bravely. The example of successful warriors would be held up to them, and the boys were urged to imitate their brave deeds.

At the time of the annual Blackfoot Medicine Lodge Ceremony, excited boys gathered by the hundreds to see the brave warriors count their coups. A man would get up holding in one hand a bundle of small sticks, and taking one from the bundle, would recount a brave deed, repeating this for each of his coups until the sticks were gone. As soon as he sat down, another man took his place. When the boys saw how respected those men were, they said to themselves, "That man was once a boy like us, and we, if we have strong hearts, may do as much as he has done." Understandably, it was not unusual for enthusiastic boys to steal off from the camp and follow war parties. In such cases they went without the knowledge of their parents and without food or extra moccasins. But aided by sympathetic older men who had done the same thing, they would get to the edge of the enemy's camp, watch the ways of the fighters, learn about going to war, and how to act when on the war trail so as to be successful. They also became acquainted with the country, and were soon equipped to undertake their adult raids.

Bearing all of this in mind, whenever a writer states that Native American boys were "not trained," he means they were not formally trained, since as one follows the course of their growth he soon begins to wonder whether, in fact, any youngster of any land ever had a better preparation for his life and environment. Throughout his early years he was instructed and groomed in religion, ethics, heritage, warfare, raiding, and hunting. Listening, observing, participating in games of skill and fortitude, practicing the techniques of running, swimming, dancing, shooting, riding, trailing, and hunting all equipped him for the proud role of a mystic warrior, and more hopefully, of a leader.

The Crow boy learned early in life that the arenas for achieving

Scout tracking enemy.

success were the fasting place, the raid, and the council of chiefs. Everything in his schooling was designed to make him yearn to begin the series of offices which made him first a war party's helper, then a scout, then a leader of scouts, then a pipeholder, and finally a chief and a head chief. Yet rarely was the progression truly as regimented as the ladder of achievement implied, for an outstanding exploit or a notably powerful vision could land a man almost anywhere on the ladder in a moment.

To become a pipeholder, or "the One Who Owns the War Party," the primary requirement was either a successful vision, which the accredited pipeholders would accept, or the purchase of an acknowledged pipeholder's war medicine bundle. However, a Crow man must also have completed the four prescribed coups even to be eligible for this office. Therefore, the boy's goal was to obtain them, and so he set out to strike an enemy with something held in his hand, to steal an enemy's best horse, to capture an enemy's weapons or medicine, and finally to ride a foe down.

There was always much to dream about, much to prepare for.

At the age of fourteen or fifteen, a promising youth might be invited to join one of the important Warrior Societies. Before he was seventeen, he might steal an enemy's horse or count coup and take a scalp. Often, before he was nineteen, his first Sun Dance would be made. At twenty he might have proven his abilities, holiness, and power sufficiently well to lead a small war party. At twenty-five he might be a chief. At the age of thirty his active warpath days would begin to draw to a close. Hopefully, he would now have many war honors and horses. He might even have two tipis, with a wife or more in each, and several children.

After thirty-five he would devote himself to the hunt, to whatever defensive warfare was required of his village, to spiritual meditations, to becoming a wise and recognized elder, and to intense concern over the future of the tribe. He would constantly substantiate his claims by the material evidence of his past achievements, for much of his time would be spent in encouraging young men to seek the warpath, and by this to perpetuate the system and his own status. Finally, the circle of life which moved along the Sacred Path would be completed, and having become "a child again," he would return to the Father Who gave him birth.

> My son, I like to have you come out with me, and travel about over the country. You have no father to teach you, and I am glad to take you with me, and to tell you the things that I know. It is a good thing to be a member of our tribe, and it is a good thing to belong to a good family in that tribe. You must always remember that you come of good people. Your father was a brave man, killed fighting bravely against the enemy. I want you to grow up to be a brave man and a good man. You must love your relations, and must do everything you can for them. If the enemy should attack the village, do not run away; think always first of defending your own people.
>
> Do you know why your relations treat you well? It is because you are a man and must act a man's part. They know that perhaps they may not have you long with them, that at any moment you may be taken away.
>
> Grinnell, *When Buffalo Ran,* pp. 35-36)

Thus far the intercommunity living, religion, arts, and weapons necessary to a boy's basic training have been considered. Now the maturing youth journeys forth to engage the challenging world around him, and those who accompany him discover what a man can accom-

Left, scout on horseback wearing buffalo hide to appear like buffalo to anyone watching from a distance. *Right*, scout with wolfskin on head looking for signs of enemy.

plish who lives in the very atmosphere of God and nature.

With the exception of the Australian aborigines, no one else has matched the abilities of the Native American as a trailer of animals and men, or his ability to survive in a land of challenging extremes. A Native American youth on the Plains may not have had reading and writing and arithmetic to learn, but he had the alphabet and calculations of the wilderness to conquer, and that alone involved the learning of a thousand signs, any combination of which must be read and acted upon immediately in order that he might triumph and live.

By the time he entered his teens, the Native American boy not only saw things non-Native Americans missed, but he saw them when they were farther away. When he couldn't see them he could put his ear to the ground and find them by their sounds. Beyond that, he could smell almost as well as the wolf. He was always at attention, looking, calculating, and measuring his chances of success. He was honed by his elders until his reactions were sharp and instant. Panic was out. When caught off guard he must automatically spot the enemy, estimate what would happen next, whether he should fight or run, and above all think more of giving warning to others than of saving himself.

The youth in training learned that an incredible number of questions faced a warrior journeying away from his home. For example, what terrain should he follow into or out of unfamiliar country? What should he do when he was about to collapse from want of water while crossing a desert? How would he obtain meat when he found himself with a broken bow or no arrows in a country filled with game? How would he know what tribe of Native Americans made a certain trail? How many were in the band, what errand were they on, were they going to or coming back from it, how far from home were they, were their horses laden, how many horses did they have and why, how many women accompanied the men, what mood were they all in? How old was the trail, where were the other Native Americans now, and what did the product of all these answers require of the sign reader? Amazing deductions from such sign reading are recorded, and would have seemed impossible if they were not so routinely faced and solved. A branch floated past him down a stream. A quick look and he would say whether this was a natural occurrence or the work of animals, or of Native Americans and trappers. Another branch, a bush, or a pebble was out of place along the trail, and he usually knew why. Off on the limits of the plain, blurred by a heat mirage, off against the gloom of distant cottonwoods, between the branches of a tree or in a cleft where a hill and mountain met, there was a split-second movement—and he knew whether man or animals made it, and why those who made it moved. When buffalo were shifting their position downwind or an elk was in an unlikely place or posture, when too many magpies were hollering at once, when a wolf's howl was off key—it always meant that something important was happening and the sign reader should govern himself accordingly.

Even as the Native American's mind was dealing with all of these factors, it was simultaneously performing a more complex judgment still. It was recording the immediate details in relation to past experiences of the country, the route across it, and the weather forecast. A ten-mile trip was always weighed in its relationship to a goal hundreds of miles away, and as such there were economics of time, effort, comfort, and horseflesh to be arranged, and success and survival would certainly depend on how well these were provided for. All this and more required continual checking as the warrior practiced his arts as hunter, soldier, tribal leader, responsible father, and craftsman. The result at the peak of his maturity was an amazing integration of faculties, a fact which soon became more than apparent to those who invaded his country, suffered where he lived comfortably, and died where he had never been in permanent danger.

One of the most unusual and yet needed abilities of the Native American was his natural faculty of direction, heightened, honed, and whetted by instructors and experience. In sheer amazement over the talents of his Native American guide, Captain R. B. Marcy wrote that he could "start from any place to which he had gone by a sinuous route, through an unknown country, and keep a direct bearing back to the place of departure; and he assured me that he never, even during the most cloudy or foggy nights, lost the points of compass. There are very few white men who are endowed with these wonderful faculties, and those few are only rendered proficient by a comparable experience." (Dodge, *33 Years Among Our Wild Indians,* pp. 551-73)

It was the exalted pipeholder's responsibility to guide the war party under all conditions. So the young Native American with ambition to

An encounter to be avoided.

succeed had to develop an exceptional sense—an instinct—of direction. And he was taught to manage this without the use of a compass. Astounding as it may seem, with a point of destination fixed in his mind, a Native American warrior could go to it as directly in darkness as in daylight, on a calm, cloudy day as well as in bright sunshine, and with the wind shifting regularly so as to blow from different quarters. His instinct could be trusted as absolutely as that of the homing goose, for he relied on what was fixed in his mind by field experience more than he did on celestial bodies or winds or landscape features.

There was no "north" and no "south" to him insofar as traveling was concerned. The Native American spoke of "sunrise" to designate that side of the horizon on which the sun rises, and of the "sunset" on the other side. He had the six ceremonial directions radiating out from any ritual circle he was in in his camp, yet he made little use of these for his journeys since the sun never rose in exactly the same place, and as such would not have been a safe guide.

The same held true for night travel. If it ever occurred to him in ancient days that use might be made of the stars to aid his journey, he dispensed with the idea. For short excursions, say for hunts of just a week or more out from his camp, he simply relied upon his conditioned instinct—not precisely the same incomprehensible something that takes a pigeon to its nest, but very close to it. In all his thirty-three years on the Plains, Colonel Dodge heard of but one instance where an Native American became "turned round," lost, and wandered for several weeks alone before he recovered himself. (Dodge, p. 551)

However, on long journeys to selected sites the warrior's primary reliance was placed upon his memory of "landmarks" he'd learned himself or been taught by others. As monotonous as the hillocks and valleys of the Plains appeared to the uneducated eye, each had its own distinctive features to him, and once the Native American had seen these, they were never forgotten. A journey into an unknown area was preceded by consultations with warriors who had already visited it, and Whites who listened to the warriors as they gave instructions said it was astonishing to see how clearly the one described and the other comprehended all that was necessary for a successful journey.

Among the Comanches, whenever neophyte braves wished to go on a raid into a country unknown to them, it was customary for some of the older men to assemble the group for instruction a day or two before the start. The youths were seated in a circle, and a bundle of sticks marked with notches to represent days was produced. Commencing with a stick with a single notch, the older warriors placed each stick in succession along a travel line, the end result being a rude map in the dirt which marked the distance to be covered each day. After a stick was placed, the larger rivers and streams which would be encountered on the next day's journey were indicated, as were the hills, valleys, ravines, and hidden water holes in dry countries. Every natural object, especially those which were peculiar or easily remembered, was located and marked. Once a given day's lesson was thoroughly understood, the stick representing the next day's march was used in the same way, and so on to the end of however many days the journey would take. A Comanche raiding party of young men and boys, the oldest being not over nineteen, and none of whom had ever been to Mexico, was known to have started from the main camp on Brady Creek in Texas and gone as far into Mexico as the city of Monterey, solely employing information fixed in their minds and

A wounded mountain lion was a dangerous prey.

represented by such sticks. Countless journeys such as this were made by groups from all Native American tribes into countries utterly strange to anyone but their elders or ancestors before the trip was made.

A party exploring a country unknown to it, or to others of the tribe, would, if it proved desirable as a hunting ground, set up small piles of stones to indicate the best route to be taken by those who followed. Numerous rock cairns were found on the rough ground of the Laramie plains of Wyoming, in the precipitous canyons of southern Kansas, and in the country north of the North Platte River. It is believed that the taller ones were built to indicate the location of the trail when the ground was covered with snow.

Society, band, or clan signs were commonly used to mark a trail—not only that others might follow, but so that all might speedily find their way back home when pursued. In the few wooded areas, trees were blazed by notching or peeling off the bark. At times young saplings were bent to the ground in an elbow shape, and instructional items such as straight sticks were tied to them. Tufts of tall grass might be bunched, tied, and bent in the direction of the trail. Piles of stones were also used on occasion where the best trails led up a steep cliff or hill. It is said that some of these stones accumulated because of the custom of the Native American, when approaching a steep grade, of picking up and throwing a stone ahead; an exercise he claimed would keep him from feeling tired.

Each of the Plains tribes had a comparatively well-defined home country which they learned by heart. Every ridge and valley was intimately known. Every shallow rut affording safety in retreat, every water hole, no matter how hidden in rocks or prairie, was indelibly marked in their mind.

Yet even in one's own country the war parties of another tribe might be encountered at any moment, so one always moved cautiously—even when close to his own camp. Sooner or later, those who failed to do so would probably be found dead. So a young man in training learned that a warrior did not walk boldly over the top of a hill, he crept to the crest and peered beyond it to see whether other men were in sight, or how the animals were acting, or else he just sat quietly like a wolf for a long time. In crossing a wide flat, a man on foot or horseback was to bend over and cover himself with his robe so that anyone seeing him from a distance might think he was a buffalo. The boy was taught that White men walked on the ridges where traveling was easy, but the wise Native American always chose the gullies. As one Native American said, "The White people think that because they cannot see Native Americans, there are none about; and this belief has caused many White people to be killed."

A youth in training soon learned to make camp at sunset, to build his fire and eat there, and then to move some distance away in the darkness to a sleeping place in the bushes where he would build no fire. In that way an enemy who watched him make the first camp would be foiled when he tried to take him by surprise.

While he could do so amazingly well, the Native American traveled comparatively little by night. Yet when advancing toward an enemy whom he hoped to surprise, when stealing horses or escaping from too close a pursuit, he overcame his natural distaste for night travel. In the average instance, however, a man on a raid wanted all the light he could get, and a prudent enemy guarded his best horses especially well during the full

Blackfoot warriors scouting for enemy sign at water's edge.

of the moon in May or June.

Every father or uncle who educated a boy was a strict disciplinarian and a good teacher. When the young man left the tipi in the morning, he would say, "Look closely to everything you see"; and at evening, on his return, he would often question the boy for an hour or so.

He would expect him to know which side of the trees had the lighter-colored bark, and which side had the most regular branches. He would ask him to name all the new birds he had seen during the day. And the boy would name them according to the color of the feathers, or the shape of the bill, or their song, or the appearance and locality of the nest. When the boy made errors, the father or uncle corrected him. There were many such questions about many things, and while a correct reply to all the questions was not immediately necessary, the intent was to make the youngster an observant and good student of nature.

Admonitions always followed the questions. A boy was told to study animals unobserved, since he would learn many of their secrets this way. A father would tell his son that he ought to follow the example of the wolf, for even when he was surprised and ran for his life, the wolf would pause to take one more look at his enemy before he entered his final retreat. The wolf also knew how to endure under the severest conditions. Deer would teach the boy how to withstand thirst for a long time. The hawks gave lessons in how to strike with unerring accuracy. The elk taught gallantry, the frogs watchfulness, the owls night wisdom and gentle ways, the bears strength and the proper use of herbs, the kit foxes cunning, the coyotes how to elude capture, and the crows how to move swiftly to the battlefield. So the boy should take a long and second look at everything he saw.

The father armed his son against the larger beasts by teaching him how to outwit them. He was to be guided by the habits of the animal he sought. A moose or elk stayed in swampy or low land or between high mountains near a spring or lake for thirty to sixty days at a time. Large game moved about continually, except the doe in the spring; it was then an easy matter to find her with her fawn.

Whenever a bear or a wildcat showed signs of attacking him, he must make the animal fully understand that he had seen him and was aware of his intentions. If he was not well equipped for a pitched battle, the only sure way to make one retreat was to take a long, sharp-pointed pole for a spear and rush toward him. No wild beast would face this unless he was cornered and already wounded. He was generally afraid of the common weapon of the larger animals—the horns, and would have learned the hard way that if these were very long and sharp, he dared not risk an open fight. Sometimes, though, a grizzly bear would attack without reason, and the only hope was to get in close and stab him repeatedly in the belly or chest. A boy was also taught that because of certain beliefs about bears, their hide could only be kept by Bear Cultists and medicine men, but any warrior could cut the claws off and wear them as a necklace.

A trainee learned that packs of gray wolves would also attack fiercely when very hungry. But even then their courage depended upon their numbers. One or two of them would never attack a man. Also, the mountain lion would attack savagely when wounded, and tracking one with an arrow in him was a very dangerous business.

The Native American boy learned how to make a number of inge-

Tracking and survival signs. *a,* Native American mounting from right side of horse. *b,* tracks at side of hoofprints indicated whether rider was Native American or White. *c,* rock moved indicated someone passed by. *d,* actions of soaring bird revealed person moving below, and bird with mud in mouth was coming from water. e, grazing mustang indicated water within three miles, and mustangs walking steadily were moving toward water. *f,* scout peering over crown of hill to avoid being seen. *g,* footprint with fresh insect lines across it indicated man passed by the night before. *h,* animal tracks of deer and wolf.

nious traps and snares to capture small animals such as badgers, foxes, coyotes, and skunks—although these were only employed when buffalo were scarce.

The larger animals such as deer and elk were to be hunted mostly in winter, and would be captured through a careful knowledge of their signs. Deer were caught at water holes, or by a knowledge of their bed-ground habits, or by calling them with a calling horn. The Shoshone fathers taught their sons to kill antelope by running them until they dropped from exhaustion. They also learned that white-tailed deer could be caught with rawhide loops placed along their trails through the willows. Winter hunters ran deer into snowdrifts, and the Native American hunters learned to make good use of dogs as bloodhounds and pack animals.

The boy was taught to recognize every animal on the Plains by its tracks, and further still to know by these exactly what it had been doing. A feeding deer moved slowly and wandered about—which was easily confirmed by finding the trodden places where one had eaten. Sand thrown up in piles meant that fawns had been playing. Sharp, spread-out tracks meant that the animal was running full tilt when it passed, and that one should forget about catching it in that vicinity.

No two animals ever left the same trail, and even beyond that, each one at each stage of its life left a trail as distinctive as the creature's appearance. The tracks told what animal it was, when it passed, its size, its mood, its age, and sometimes its sex. So when following tracks, one never walked on them, but alongside to preserve them for further reference.

A Plains science of great consequence was the ability to read an animal's droppings. Once he had acquired this skill, a Native American hunter could tell exactly what species of animal had dropped it, and by the size of the pellets whether it was a large or small specimen of its kind. Piled pellets meant the creature was not being molested at the time it dropped them, while scattered ones showed that it was racing away.The consistency and temperature told the hunter a great deal about the animal's whereabouts. He could see what it was eating, and look for the source. In winter a still steaming sign meant the game was near. Cold pellets were dropped an hour before, and the animal might already be a mile or so away. Frozen pellets indicated that the game was probably two or more miles distant.

Northern tribes were seldom faced with an acute water problem, but in an arid southern wilderness, shortages could easily become the most serious hazard of all for travelers. Ancient stories attest to the anxiety, the suffering, and the tragedy exacted by a Plains land of little water or widely spaced water holes.

Wherever he was, a first requirement was that by merely looking at the country, a warrior should be able to judge accurately in what direction water could be found and the approximate distance to it.Therefore, he had to be familiar with every grass, shrub, bird, or animal that indicated water in a general way. Even more, he must know the significance of all the vegetation and animal life of a particular country he ranged. By these he often estimated his elevation and his approximate location in relation to familiar landmarks.

A hundred years ago one could have blindfolded and taken an experienced Native American warrior anywhere in the Plains country, then uncovered his eyes so that he could look at the vegetation, and he

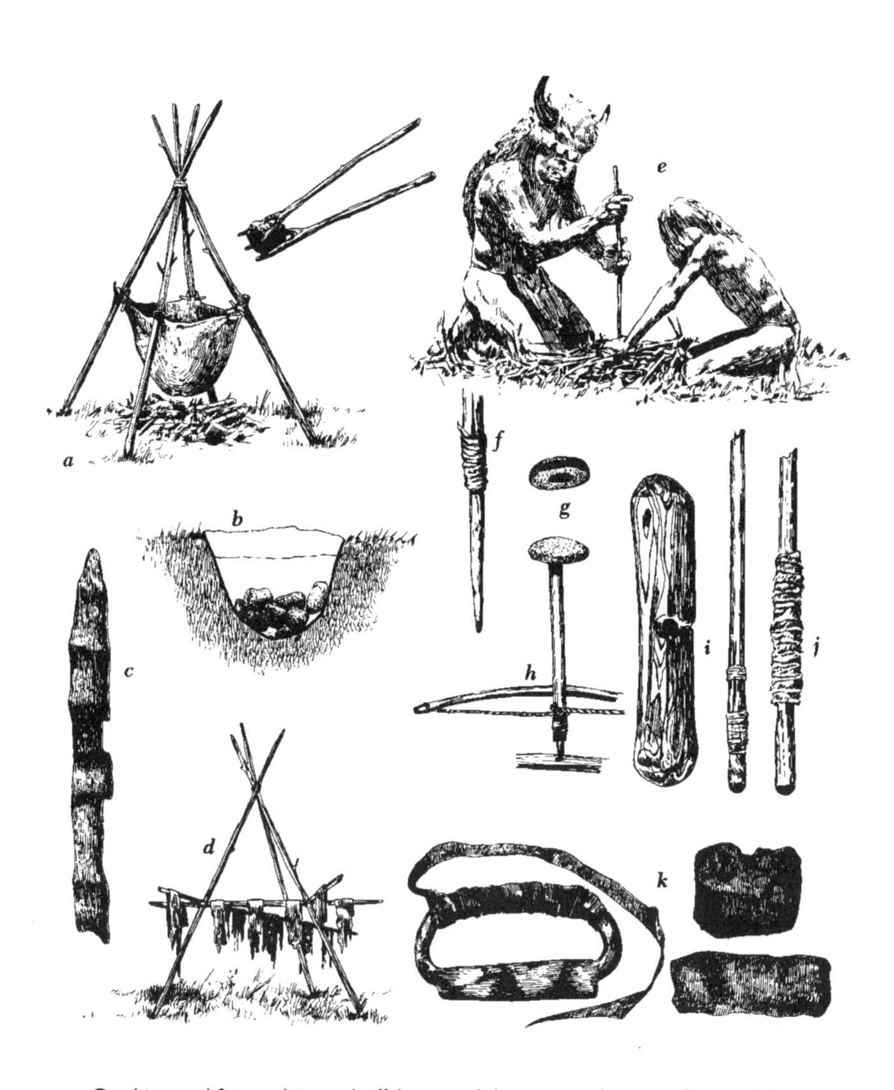

Cooking and fire making. *a,* buffalo paunch hung on poles over fire, and also showing how heated rocks were carried on forked sticks to be dropped in water in paunch. *b,* buffalo paunch used to line pit dug in ground. *c,* meat sliced thin for jerky. *d,* small rack built to dry jerky while traveling. e, two men working together to spin fire drill. *f,* Crow wooded drill point, *g,* stone cap to protect hand. *h,* bow drill. *i,* Lehmi Shosone hearth and drill. *j.* Wind River Shosone drill. *k,* flints and steel carried by a Sioux warrior.

could have told where he was. The southern mesquite, for instance, had different forms for varying altitudes, latitudes, and areas of aridity. It did not grow far north of where old Toscosa now is in the Texas Panhandle. And while there were many mesquites adjacent to the Canadian River in the Panhandle of Texas, a few miles away one would find only a few lonesome bushes on great sections of land. So a Native American scouting on the Plains was always glad to see a mesquite bush, for in the dry climate it sprang up only from the droppings of an animal, and the only one that ate mesquite seeds was the mustang. After the mesquite seeds were soaked for a while in the bowels of a horse and were dropped, they germinated quickly. The Native American scout knew that undisturbed mustangs rarely grazed out from water more than three miles. Therefore, when a mesquite bush was seen, all he had to do was to locate the direction of the water.

Cottonwood trees always indicated water, and the Native American boy was taught that when he saw a long line of cottonwoods before him, he would know that if there was water the entire length, the foliage of all the trees would be the same dark color. If the water was only in holes, the trees near these holes would be much darker, and it was useless to hunt the length of the line when nature's signs were so clear. Sometimes a tule—a water grass—showed where water had sunk into a bed of heavy wet sand. By riding his horse up and down this bed of sand he could, with luck, cause the water to rise.

When a Native American youth was familiar with every bird of the region, he would know those that watered each day, like the dove, and those that could go without water for a long while, like the Mexican quail. A careful observer could mark the course of the doves as they went off each evening into the breaks to water. But the easiest of all the birds to follow was the dirt dauber or swallow. He flew low and straight, and if his mouth was empty he was going to water. If his mouth had mud in it, he was coming straight from water. The Native American could also watch the animals, and learn from them where water was. Mustangs watered daily, at least in the summertime, while antelope sometimes went for months without a drop. If mustangs were strung out and walking steadily along, they were going to water. If they were scattered, frequently stopping to graze, they were coming from water.

In some southern areas, water was very scarce, and in many places it was extremely bad. In fact, most of it was undrinkable, for it often had a sickening effect. In these areas the Native Americans sometimes suffered exceedingly from thirst, which suffering was said to be the worst torture of all. At night they tossed in a semiconscious slumber in which they dreamed of every spring they knew. The restlessness invariably awakened them, leaving them in even more distress. Suffering from thirst caused a strange reaction. Every ounce of moisture was sapped from the flesh, leaving men and animals haggard and thin, so that one could hardly recognize them if they had been deprived for a long time.

Given half a chance, however, the Native Americans learned how to take care of themselves in such dire emergencies. Placing a small pebble in the mouth would help, a bullet was better, a piece of copper, if obtainable, better yet, and a peeled piece of prickly pear was the best of all. To drink muddy water, a warrior put grass over the surface to strain out the flies or bugs, and sucked the water through it.

Under any and all conditions the Native American boy had to learn to be able to make a fire. He needed it for warmth, and he needed it to

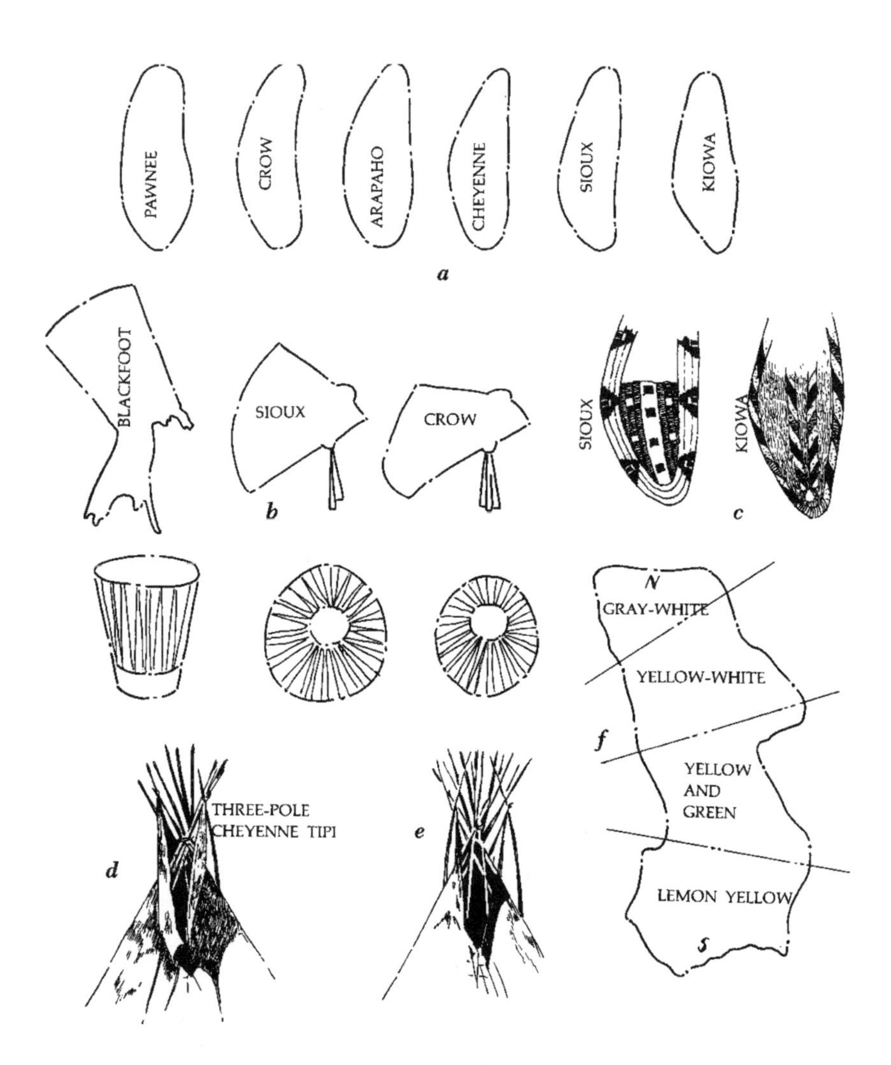

Signs used by raiders to identify enemies from a distance. *a*, footprints of different tribes—from right to left, Kiowa, Sioux, Cheyenne, Arapaho, Crow, Pawnee. *b*, side and back shapes of feathered headdresses—from left to right, Blackfoot, Sioux, Crow. *c*, southern Plains moccasins with strong diagonal pattern, northern moccasins with mountain designs. *d*, three-pole tipi used by Cheyenne. *e*, four-pole tipi used by Crows. *f*, clothing color division of Plains area—from north to south, gray-white, yellow-white, yellow and green, lemon yellow.

cook his food. It is true that some portions of a newly slain animal were eaten raw, such as the liver and some fats, and in emergencies the gall was drunk and the raw lining of the second stomach was eaten, but the common practice was to cook whatever was not to be "jerked" for future use.

Whenever possible, cooking was done in a buffalo paunch, the animal's stomach lining. This served as a kettle or bucket to hold the water for boiling the meat. The paunch was suspended from four green poles, each about five feet long. Small wooden pegs pinned the edges to the poles.

The paunch was washed and half filled with water, and the meat was placed in it. Carefully selected clean stones, chosen for their resistance to cracking or exploding, were piled on a log framework above a fire located to one side of the paunch, heated till they were red-hot, and then dropped one at a time into the paunch. The water was kept at a continual boil, and it cooked the meat in about thirty minutes. The broth made a very good soup, and the kettle itself could be eaten once the primary meal was finished.

When hunters were without poles to hold the paunch, they dug a hole in the ground and placed the paunch in it. For fuel to heat the stones they used buffalo chips. These were the prime fuel of the Plains, for they remained dry in the center when wet by rain, they burned slowly, and they made a hot fire with more glow than flame.

To preserve their meat, the Native Americans "jerked" it. To do this, they cut it into very thin slices, a quarter of an inch or less thick and from one to six feet long. The thin slices were placed on wooden racks and dried in about two days. They were not smoked. Flies were unable to plant their eggs in the thin meat, and so left it alone. In drying, the meat became very hard. It could be eaten in that condition, but was usually cooked before meals taken at home. Warriors on the move ate it without cooking it while they were in enemy country. A small tripod rack was used by war or hunting parties to dry the meat slices. Huge drying racks literally covered the main camp areas during the hunting seasons.

Pemmican was the other best-known type of prepared meat. To make it, jerky was pounded to a fine consistency with a berrymasher. Fresh chokecherries were then pounded to a pulp and mixed with the jerky. Suet was poured on this, and the whole was divided into small cakes which were stored in rawhide cases for future use.

The ancient way of making fire on the Plains was by the "fire stick" friction of wood on wood. The end of a round stick was split, and a hardwood point was inserted in the split and lashed tight. Then the stick, called a "drill," was twirled between the palms of the hands while the turning end spun and ground on another piece of wood called the "hearth." This was done by a single man, or better by two men working in relays. Friction caused the wood to form a hot powder or glowing coal, which was allowed to fall into a tinder. To coax this into a flame the Native American blew softly on it or placed it in a "sling" of grass or strip of bark and swung it back and forth in the air.

An improvement over that method came when the Native American began using a bow with a thong of soft rawhide, which was turned once around the drill stick, and as the bow was run back and forth, the thong spun the stick. The drill stick was held at the top by a cupped-out stone, a piece of wood, or a clamshell to protect the fire maker's hand

Blackfoot warriors Black Bull and Stabs by Mistake searching countryside for sign of enemies.

while he pressed down on it to hold it against the hearth.

It is said that some tribes believed that a spark of fire "slept" only in certain kinds of trees, and only the roots of these were to be used in kindling a flame by friction.

The tinders used were dried wood from decayed trees, frayed inner bark of the cedar, fungi, pounded buffalo chips, or downy feathers of the blue jay. The Blackfoot tribes used a fungus which grows on the birch tree, gathering it in large quantities and drying it so as always to have it available to start their fires. Of course, the flints and steels of the Whites were more sure and provided an instant spark, so at almost their first meeting with the traders the Native Americans obtained flints and steels and enthusiastically learned how to use them.

In a common method of transportation, fire was carried from camp to camp in a "fire horn." This was a large buffalo horn with its core burnt out, and slung by a buckskin loop over the shoulder like a powder horn. The horn was lined with moist, rotten wood, and the open end had a hardwood stopper or plug fitted to it. On leaving camp in the morning, the man who had the responsibility of carrying the horn took a live coal from the fire and put it in the horn. On this coal he placed a piece of punk, and then plugged up the horn with the stopper. The punk smoldered in this almost airtight chamber, and after the course of two or three hours, the man looked at it, and if it was nearly consumed, put another piece of punk in the horn. The first men who reached the appointed camping place would gather several large piles of wood in different places, and as soon as the one who carried a fire horn reached camp, he turned out his spark at one of these piles of wood. A little blowing and nursing resulted in the blaze which started the fire. All other fires of a village were kindled from this first one, and when the rest of the party reached camp they went to these blazing piles for coals with which to start the fires in their lodges.

If trailing animals had its adventures, even these took on a heightened dimension when the competition was elevated to one between hunter and hunter, skilled man against skilled man—and both were products of the same schoolroom! One could never be certain as to which in any case had the advantage over the other as they traveled on the prairies.

The Native Americans of one tribe knew that their enemies depended on the same landmarks they relied upon for their own guides, and as they trailed them they might even be able to determine where the others were headed and take a short cut to intercept them. On the other hand, the enemies might turn back and do the same to them.

Boys were taught that by moccasin tracks a Native American tracker *might* determine the identity of the tribe of the man who made them. Nearly every tribe had its own pattern and method of decorating moccasins, so that under ideal conditions it was possible for a skilled Native American scout to tell a man's tribe by a study of their tracks. Captain William F. Drannan, who spent thirty-one years on the Plains and in the mountains, and many of them with Kit Carson, declares that no two tribes cut and made their moccasins alike, and at that time he could tell a Native American by his track—"if he belonged to any tribe he was familiar with." (Drannon, *Thirty-One Years on the Plains,* p. 255) The toe and heel shapes of the various tribes did differ, but all moccasins toed in, and a print could seldom be read without an absolutely clear and crisp track, for the variations were not that great. The Native Ameri-

Warriors picking up fallen comrade by use of rope in midst of battle.

cans themselves were often not able to identify a track they found. They stated that their war parties found some tracks, but "they did not know whose they were." (Linderman, *Plenty Coups,* p. 247)

Travelers also employed tricks to deceive potential pursuers. They usually walked over rough ground, and warriors picked up enemy moccasins from victims whenever they could to wear when they entered that tribe's territory. Some Native Americans put an animal tail or a heavy fringe at the heel of their moccasins, which was said to obliterate or smear the tracks as the wearer walked along.

An experienced tracker *could* tell whether the man he was after was running or walking. If he was running, only the ball of his foot touched the ground. If the fugitive was trying to throw his pursuer off the trail by walking backward, his steps were of necessity shorter, his heel marks were deeper, and the trained pursuer would notice this.

A young man learned to tell a great deal from the tracks and other evidences of animals, and he was taught to put the same principles to work on the natural objects. If he saw a rock moved from its regular place, he could tell when it was moved by the edges of the dirt, for the wind changed these hour by hour. If he saw a broken twig, a broken blade of grass, or a bit of weed cut off by a horse's hoof, he was able to tell exactly how long it had been withering. It was easy to determine whether a track had been made before or after daylight. A track made during the night would usually be marked with minute insect tracks. Even on desert sands this was true. By bending close to the ground, the scout could observe the tiny insect lines.

The Native American trailer must become alert to everything. If the one he pursued did not leave traces, the trailer still might determine the direction in which other men were going by noting the tracks of animals frightened out of their path. Flocks of birds rising swiftly and sharply showed that someone was moving and frightening them.

When a man was away from home every living thing was watched for any significance attached to its motion or appearance. No movement was too slight for the hunter to ignore, and no sound too meaningless to go unheeded. The soaring maneuvers of any bird were to be looked into. If a man was below an eagle, the bird would either circle over him or turn back and fly the other way. The calls of the prairie cranes were announcers of important weather changes. Herman Lehmann tells how Comanche Indians could forecast the weather by examining the webs of spiders. In dry weather the web was thin, long, and high, but just before a rain the web was low, short, and thick. A croaking frog proclaimed a tiny marsh or hidden spring, and at once called for more caution. Someone might already be there. A distant dust column might reveal an advancing enemy party.

Even the black horned ground beetle, commonly called the tumblebug, was attentively watched. The two horns on the top of the insect's head were movable in all directions, yet they were invariably pointed and held toward a buffalo herd, probably being attracted in that direction by the noise made by stamping hoofs too distant even for sensitive human ears.

If a fugitive tried to cover his tracks by wading up or down a stream, the trailer was taught first to look for the trail on the same side of the water where the other man had entered it. Usually a man would come out of the water on the same side. But there was always the question of whether he had done this deliberately or through force of habit, and so the trailer had to reason out whether he had a cunning or a thoughtless man to deal with. Miscalculations were exceedingly dangerous, for often the pursuer, being outwitted, found himself being pursued or ambushed instead.

A successful warrior's hearing must be sharpened until it was perfect. Reading sounds correctly had much to do with his longevity as a scout, since the enemy was as expert as he at animal and bird imitations. The Native Americans often used these to locate and orient themselves at night. But it is said that no man's imitation cry of a bird or beast could actually deceive a skilled hunter.

The Native Americans discovered that the human voice echoes more than any other; in truth, it is almost the only voice which echoes at all. Of course, on the open plains of northeast Texas, the Native Americans did not have this advantage because there was nothing to create an echo. But the ancient Native Americans who were consulted about the mountains, canyons, and broken country agreed that no human could give an exact imitation of the sound of a beast or bird there. A Crow Indian declared that he easily knew when the enemy was gathering in strength. "All night long coyote yelps and wolf howls in the hills indicated that they were closing in." When owls were heard in addition, he knew that Sioux, Cheyenne, and Arapaho were thick about his party "like ants on a freshly killed buffalo hide." (Linderman, p. 165)

An expert trailer could readily tell whether a pony was carrying anything by the depth of its tracks. Also, the position of the hoofmarks would show whether the pony was walking, trotting, or galloping.

The experienced Native American tracker could tell whether a horse track had been made by a loose horse, a riderless horse being led, or a horse with a man riding him. He could even determine the horse's color. Suppose he was on the hunt for a man he knew to be riding a brown horse. He found the tracks of a horse carrying a man. But was the horse a brown horse? To determine this he simply followed the tracks until he found where the rider had unsaddled his mount to let him graze. When the saddle was taken off, a horse that had been ridden any distance generally fell on the ground. When the tracker found where the one he was trailing had rolled, he examined the dirt or the grass for hairs, found a few, and their color told him whether the horse was brown. Another fact was that no Native American wore boots, so that footprints easily showed whether the rider was Native American or White. The Native American warrior usually mounted and dismounted on the right side of the horse because he carried his weapons in his right hand,

a
b

Signaling methods. *a,* using robe or blanket with horse standing still. *b,* robe used in combination with moving horse. *c,* using mirror. *d,* smoke signals.

and did not then need to throw them across the horse's back. The White man mounted and dismounted on the left side. In considering the absoluteness of always mounting on the right side, an amused old Blackfeet warrior claimed that his horse was trained to receive him from any direction in an emergency—even over the rear end if necessary, since anything else would have accounted for "a heap of dead Indians!"

It was important for the boy in training to be taught how the Native Americans of different tribes could tell one another apart, and especially how they could tell friend from foe in the haste and fright of an unexpected confrontation, or at the sighting of a distant camp. There were a few definite signs they could go by.

Clear moccasin tracks would be one indication. A second would be the variations in tribal bonnet styles. A third sign would be the difference between the northern and southern moccasin quill or bead designs, with the southern moccasin being recognized by its strong diagonal lines. A fourth help would be the zonal color variations in garments. Northern clothing, such as that of the Blackfoot and Crees, was either a sparkling white with a gray cast, or else painted in a purple range. Next came the Crow-Sioux area. Their garments were white with a yellow cast—or else a smoked, warm beige. After this was the Cheyenne country garments, which were painted a yellow of a stronger nature than their northern neighbors', and finally the southernmost clothing color preference of lemon yellow and green. A last indication would be the difference between tipi pole structures. The Crows, for example, used a four-pole base and the Cheyenne a three-pole foundation upon which the other poles were laid.

Once the basic skills of making and handling weapons, of horsemanship, of hunting, and of survival and tracking had been conquered, a young man was ready to complete his training period by also mastering the techniques of raiding and war for tribal defense and being a member of pipeholders' war parties. Naturally, his exposure to these had been a regular part of his life from childhood, and he had continually imitated everything his father and the other warriors did, doing so by himself or in concert with other boys. Therefore, a youth about to take up the mature responsibilities of manhood did not need to learn the warring skills so much as he needed to practice with other men in order to become an efficient part of his tribe's defense unit.

In warfare and raiding the warrior remained an individual. He was always, in a sense, his own man. He answered to his supernatural helpers in that he conducted himself in accordance with instructions received in visions and dreams. He also developed a special allegiance to his society, and his conduct in the field was governed in part by the club's rules, by its aims, and by his vows to fellow members. Standing over all of this, however, was his responsibility to the band and tribe to defend it against any menace. This meant that besides the practice needed to increase an individual's proficiency with weapons, there must also be society, village, and tribal drills in readiness for those great and sudden emergencies when a large enemy war party attacked his village, or when it became desirable to strike at the enemy in force on their home grounds.

Every band or clan had its camp chiefs and its war chiefs. The latter were men who had earned their positions by superior achievements in battles, and often they were the leading officers of the various men's societies. Each of the war chiefs chose several subchiefs to assist him, and each of these were assigned a certain number of the men of the band.

Both the experienced warriors and the trainees were called out for instruction several times a week when the weather was good.

The war chiefs agreed in a general way as to what they would try to accomplish. Then each subchief gathered his unit around him and outlined the plan, and they proceeded from there.

The tactical maneuvers of the Plains tribes always presupposed an enemy located in various and strategic places. The war chiefs set the situation for their units, and at a signal sent their mounted warriors speeding toward the enemy positions, racing and circling in such a way as to confuse the enemy regarding their actual strength and plan. Warriors on foot had already mastered the skills of approaching their prey without being discovered, and in maneuvers, it was simply a matter of learning to coordinate their efforts with the other members of their unit. Ambush techniques were also considered and practiced, for this was a favorite method of attack on the Plains.

Drills included training in picking up fallen warriors while riding at top speed, each man practicing until he could do it alone, or better still with another warrior, for two men could do this surprisingly well. If a man was down but still able to move, a rope loop was dropped over his head as the pickup team rode by. While they circled, the downed man slipped his arms through the rope and got to his hands and knees. On the next pass of the pickup team, one man swung down and grabbed the loose end of the rope with his left hand while the other caught the loop with his right hand, and together they hoisted the wounded man and carried him off the field of battle to a safe place. Here, depending upon his condition, they either put him down or else took him up to ride double with them on one of the horses.

Warrior looking back to guard against pursuers.

The war chiefs signaled their men in several ways: by hand or arm signals—sometimes holding a flag or a lance or a gun or a robe at arm's length; by the use of trade mirrors; or by war whistles made of the bone of an eagle's wing or of a turkey leg bone. It is said that two different sounds could be produced by blowing each end of the whistles. Such whistles made a shrill noise, and were easily heard above the din of battle. At any signal the different units would immediately wheel or turn, attack or retreat as prearranged. As long as the practiced techniques went well in an actual battle, the prepared orders were followed—but if anything went awry, it was every man for himself until a desist or retreat sign was issued, or he decided to leave on his own.

Actually, two kinds or modes of signals were employed on the Plains—those just mentioned which were designed for close-quarter communication, and those designed for signaling over long distances of a mile or more. There were three long-distance methods: body action; action of the signaler in connection with objects, such as a robe or blanket, or a mirror, or a flag or lance, or the direction imparted to a horse; and by smoke or fire or dust. Using any of these means the Native Americans could signal alarm, anger, a request to come, warnings of danger, defiance, a call to halt, directions, peace, friendship, a question such as "Who are you?" submission, surrender, buffalo discovered, the success of a war party, a camp site, and the implementation of a military drill.

Smoke or mirror signals were used in daytime, with the number of flashes or puffs serving as a kind of Morse code, and fires placed at intervals in rows accomplished the same thing at night. Smoke signals were made by letting the smoke rise in a single column, or by slipping a robe or blanket sideways over a fire made with dry wood and green grass or moss thrown on it. Fire signals were made on high ridges or away from water so that people would know they were not campfires.

The Native Americans made horseback signals by riding in certain ways, walking, circling, zigzagging, or racing to indicate their message. Sometimes a warrior just rode into view and away again one or more times. The Omahas had a signal in which two scouts crisscrossed on their horses. Robes and blankets were added to the horseback maneuvers to convey the more complicated messages. Certain signals were given by tossing a balled-up robe into the air a given number of times. Friends were summoned by waving the robe in an outward motion and back again.

Of this much one could be sure, the boy in training learned that all the while a warrior traveled, he must realize that as he watched for others he was being just as intently spied upon. The eyes of the animal world were upon him, and human eyes would often be too. Every so often he must turn quickly to scan the landscape in back of him, and if he had reason to suspect the presence of an enemy scout, he should lay in wait until the enemy watcher was located.

When a young man's training had made him a proficient hunter and neophyte warrior, he was ready to make his first excursions into the enemy war zone. Here he reached the supreme level in his life, and discovered that spirituality and limited warfare were really not as alien as one might think for the natural man.

Young warrior challenging enemy.

The Mature Warrior on the Field of Action

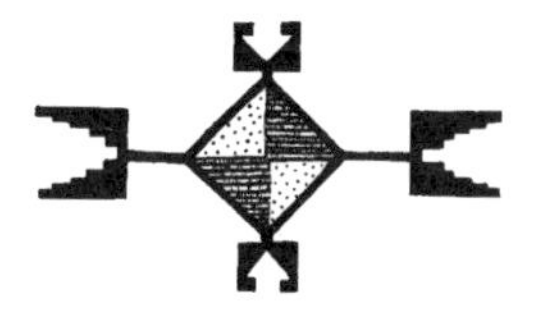

"Yes," he smiled. "I shall always remember my first war-party. I was asked to go by the man who was to carry the pipe, and I felt so proud I could scarcely keep the secret to myself. I thought the day very long, and was relieved when at night we rode silently out of the village with our faces toward the east. We wore only light shirts and leggings made from the skins of bighorns, and carried nothing except our bows and shields. War-bonnets and bright colors were hidden away, because they can be seen easily, and no war-party wishes to be seen. Bonnets were never used by warriors until all chance of surprise was gone. Then they were brought out, if there was time. Our bonnets were in rawhide cases and might not be used at all."

We rode all night without seeing our Wolves. Yet I knew, of course, they were out ahead of us somewhere. I kept looking at every knoll top until we hid away for the day. Then they came in, looking exactly like wolves."

Linderman, *Plenty Coups,* pp. 119-20

The Native American boy who lived during the golden age of the Plains people was trained from infancy to be a warrior. In a sense, his very life was oriented around the field of conquest. This fact must, however, be prefaced and tempered with a qualifying note. According to

Native American accounts, prior to the advent of the horse and mobile warfare in the 1700s, there were neither general nor continued disputes of consequence among the Plains tribes. Once each nation had settled into its geographic area, it lived on relatively good terms with its neighbors. Most quarrels were trivial at best, since there were few people, and there was plenty of land for everyone. Physical confrontations were inconsequential, since defensive skills could nearly offset the damage which could be done by the old stone weapons. The greatest losses in early times occurred when one party was surprised from ambush, or when one side panicked and ran so they could be struck from behind. If, however, the pursued party rallied and turned to fight, the pursuers usually drew off at once, well satisfied with whatever they had already accomplished. With the arrival of the horse, however, raiding and warfare became an intense manner of life for the entire tribe: the men making the raids, the women helping to prepare for their going and receiving them back, the older men aiding with exhortations, advice, and prayers, and the young learning in anticipation of their days to come. Even then casualties were usually light—because the coup, not killing, was what counted.

The Kiowas say they could never understand why the Whites made such a fuss over small fights. Fighting was a man's business—that was the way he earned the respect of his people and was honored by the women. In their eyes there never would have been any serious trouble if the Whites had stayed away and left them alone: "We were happy before they came." (Mayhall, *The Kiowas,* pp. 270-78)

Robert Lowie points out that he learned of no concerted effort by one tribe to oust another from their territory, and that tradition revealed

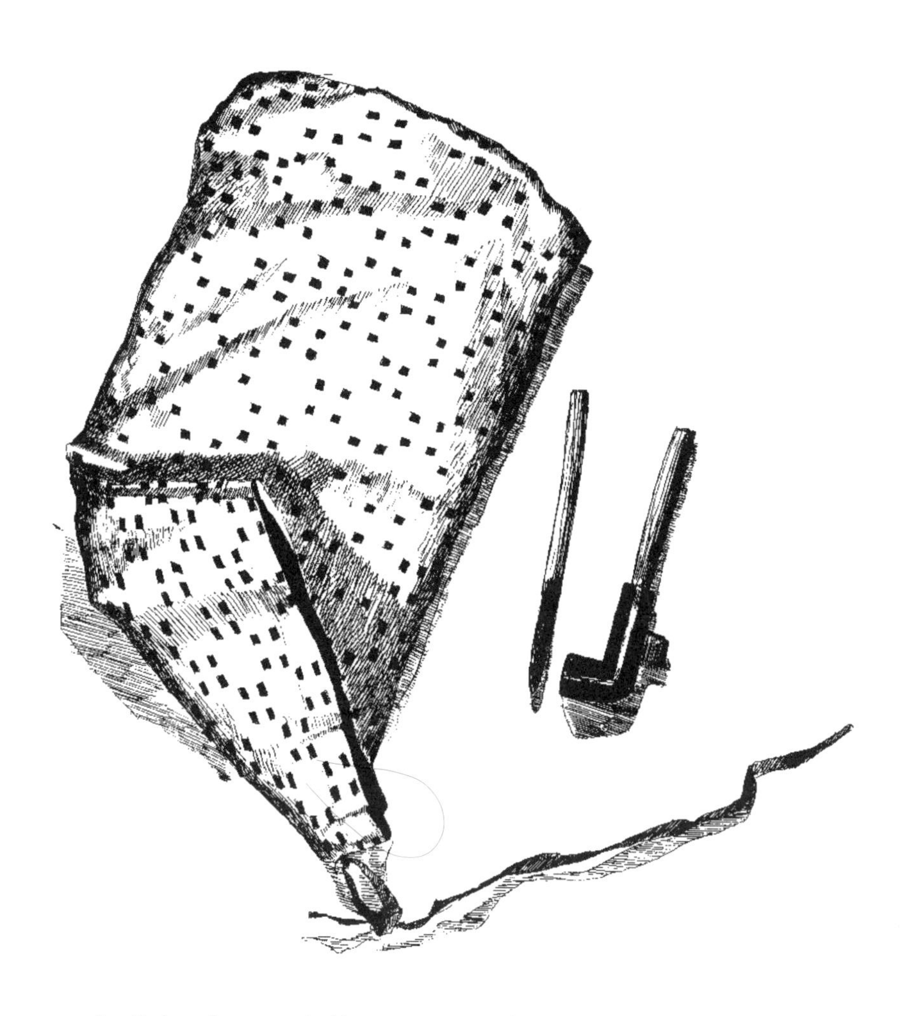

Small pipe of type carried by warrior on raid, with pipe tamper stick. Pipe is 4 1/2 inches long, stone bowl. The tobacco bag is calico, red with small yellow squares.

that relatively few wars were fought on a really large scale. (Lowie, *Indians of the Plains,* pp. 198–204)

George Grinnell felt that the White people completely misunderstood how the Native Americans enjoyed their small encounters, that it is impossible for those who live the commonplace, humdrum lives of a civilized community to form any adequate conception of the variety and excitement of the life of a young man who was constantly going on the warpath. He believed that the barest enumeration of the odd circumstances and thrilling occurrences which took place in a single band of a brave, warlike nation would fill many volumes. "Such a recital would present many examples of reckless hardihood almost beyond belief." (Grinnell, *The Story of the Indian,* pp. 125,126)

A very strong case can be made for White intrusion as the real motivation for some of the deep and lasting antagonisms which came to pass between the Native American tribes during the horse period. The White soldiers and settlers encouraged them to turn against each other, caused territorial shifts or pressures, and kept them in such a ferment over their land losses and cultural interferences that the mood of the Native American underwent a marked change. Where once war was sporadic, it became systematic. Where once it was considered sport, it became a deadly contest of counterthrust and revenge.

There were two types of trips made by the Native American warriors into enemy territory. Some journeys were for the express purpose of making war, but the most common purpose was the horse raid, and the horse alone was *the* target. Raiders rarely attacked enemy villages with the intent to destroy or appropriate other property. They took horses, and in many instances probably retrieved animals already stolen from

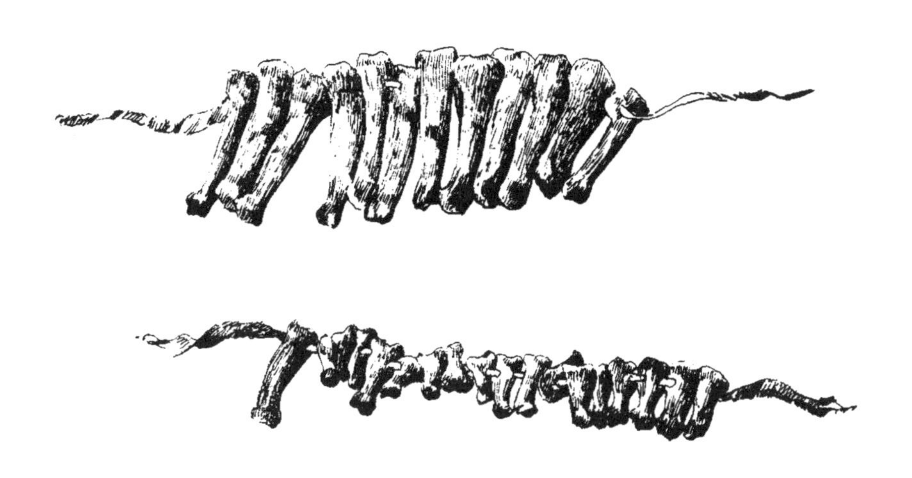

Finger-bone necklace made from fingers taken in revenge raids.

themselves. Other things were brought home on occasion. After a battle, and time permitting, some of the weapons and apparel of their enemies might be taken as proof of victory.

As a rule, horse raids were stimulated by tribal defense patterns or came about as a reaction to the activities of the enemy. Blackfoot accounts say that most raids "originated in a dream," but the aforementioned causes were undoubtedly the foster parents of the dream itself. In any case, dreams came at all times during the year, and men responded to them by going on raids during all but the impossible parts of the winter. A dream might only provide the impulse to go, but it often included an uncanny prediction of the destination, and even something of what would take place there. Significantly enough, such dreams usually came to men of proven merit, for everyone knew—and was influenced by the fact—that other men were not likely to follow an inexperienced leader into enemy territory.

If a dream inspired confidence, the warrior who had it invited certain men of proven or potential worth to accompany him—the number depending upon the task which confronted them. The invitation could be accepted, or it could be declined without embarrassment on the part of one who felt it was not a proper time for him to go. His own dream might warn him off, which was an honorable excuse during those times when raiding was an option. Tribal defense was another matter, and membership in a large war party became the obligation of every warrior within the fighting age bracket of fifteen to thirty-five. A man older than that or a medicine man could turn instead to prayers or to making medicine—as did Sitting Bull during the famous Custer affair. His contribution would be considered as important as the fighting

Pawnee war leader, back view, wearing painted buffalo robe, buffalo hair rope, otter skin collar with ear of corn and storm eagle hung on collar, and carrying lance and shield.

itself, and his prestige would not suffer.

Any raiding party could also include a few men who were not invited—especially young men anxious to get started—yet who would follow the party out and join them some distance after they left the village. These were not always the most desirable traveling mates, but they were acceptable if they were willing to submit to the authority of the party leader.

A noteworthy exception to the normal procedure occurred when certain young men became especially desirous to make a name for themselves, and decided to sneak off during a period of intertribal tensions when the elders felt that it was a time to be more prudent; when the risks and consequences were considered greater than usual. Knowing the mind of the youth from their own neophyte days, the chiefs posted society members around the camp perimeter to watch for young adventurers, and it became an interesting contest to see which could outwit the other as the adventurers attempted to sneak away. "Youth," said the Indian elders, "is like fire, marvellous to behold, but needing to be controlled." (Linderman, p. 137)

The leader of a raid or a war party became known as the pipeholder, or the one who carried the pipe. If the trip was to be a long and especially dangerous one, he would have been on many raids already, and in most instances would be well acquainted with all the landmarks and water holes in whatever country they might cross. Often the leader would be a war priest, known for his visions and astuteness. Once a man accepted the pipeholder's invitation, his authority became all but absolute, and the party put itself in his hands for preparation and execution from that moment until the day it returned home.

By and large, the approach to raiding and warfare was the same for all tribes, yet each had its peculiarities which, taken in their sum, added luster to the general picture.

Therefore, the following material is drawn from the comprehensive Native American accounts of the Sioux, Blackfoot, Crow, Kiowa, Cheyenne, Assiniboine, and Shoshone tribes. The general sequential pattern of raids will be followed, and the interesting details from each tribe will be inserted whenever they deviated from the norm. The total picture produced will portray more happenings than would take place on the ordinary raid or battle trip, yet each journey would include a significant part of them.

The Native Americans were always prayerful and careful in their religious observances, but they were never more scrupulous about these matters than when starting on a journey to war. Realizing they were risking their lives, they sought divine assistance and offered sacrifices, such as slices of flesh, in return. In most instances, a priest was asked to lead them in a medicine sweat, and while they were in the sweat lodge, he smoked the sacred pipe and prayed, asking that they might return in safety to their people. While they were away he would continue to pray for their success and welfare, and at intervals would ride about through the camp, shouting out the names of the warriors to make certain they would not be forgotten by the people whom they had gone forth to protect. One should always remember that their warfare was defensive, rather than an exercise for personal glory. The stories told by the Native Americans make constant reference to the need to protect and preserve the tribe. If it was a revenge raid, men would gash each other's legs to gird and excite themselves for the task. Sometimes a great tribal holy

Warriors scarifying (gashing) legs in fortifying attitudes for revenge raid. Lowie and Ewers reported that hoop medicines were one of the most sacred war medicine bundles carried to war, especially in revenge situations.

item would be taken along to ensure success. The Kiowas, for example, often took one of their ten sacred medicines. If it got wet at any time, everyone took it as a plain warning to turn back.

There were also mechanical things to be done, and except for the preparation for intertribal wars, these must be carried out in secret or performed casually to prevent unwanted people from learning what was happening and seeking to join the party.

The clothing worn for war parties and horse raids depended upon the nature of the job at hand. On occasion the Native American warriors rode forth bareback and near naked. But they usually were wrapped in a blanket or fully dressed in lightweight shirts and leggings. In summer these prevented sunburn, in winter they were for warmth, and in all instances they guarded the wearer against being scraped by brush, thorns, and rocks. Northern winter gear included the blanket coat called the capote, with red or yellow horizontal stripes, which made it harder for the enemy to see the coat. The finest clothing and regalia, including warbonnets and coup feathers, were carried along on war expeditions, so that time permitting they could be put on before the enemy was engaged. Most of this gear was packed in the familiar parfleche and fringed cylindrical cases and suspended from the saddle. Upon arriving in the vicinity of an enemy village, a war party put on its war clothes, took the saddles off the horses, and left all of the superfluous gear at a carefully chosen place to be picked up after the battle. War clothes were worn as indications to the enemy of a warrior's abilities, and as reminders to the owner of the medicine things he should be thinking of. A Kiowa warrior said that his war clothing was put on so as to prepare him properly for death.

War leader riding out to challenge and taunt enemy prior to rare mass battle between large groups.

An impressive amount of gear would be taken on a raid, and even more on a war party. Each warrior would provide his share of the equipment, so that between the members of a given group, everything necessary would be available as it was required. There would be rawhide carrying cases and such clothing as fitted the journey; extra bowstrings, carried in the quiver; glue sticks, carried in the quiver; quirts; a small supply of sinew and awls; war paint bags and shell cups for mixing the paint; extra moccasins, sometimes carried under the covers of the shields; fire-making equipment, the old bow types or flint and steel; jerky and pemmican; the small field pipes, wooden pipe tampers, and tobacco—with pipe bags; personal medicine items, and the special war medicine of the band; robes or blankets, sometimes rolled and strapped across the back infantry-style; bows, and perhaps extra ones for a war party trip, and about twenty arrows per man; knives, usually good-sized multipurpose ones for skinning or battle; shields if riding, but not always carried when on foot—miniature shields or just the large shield covers might be taken instead, clubs and/or tomahawks; lances, a standard weapon for mounted warfare, and certainly not unknown to foot parties either, at least in short, lightweight versions; when guns were taken, the added equipment consisted of powder horns or flasks, and patch bags for bullets or patches and round balls; enemy moccasins to deceive their pursuers; ropes to make war bridles for stolen horses; and snowshoes for rough going in winter.

All of the survival talents the Native American had mastered were called upon each step of the way out to a raid or battle and back, and in its sum, the journey to weaken the strength of the foe became an exercise in consummate skill, especially when one realizes that parties of

Foot party of warriors on winter revenge raid. State of dress and alertness show they are on border of enemy territory and have dressed for battle. Dogs were often used as pack animals. Old photo by Schultz, *My Life As an Indian,* shows Blackfoot war party in winter dressed as group shown in drawing.

warriors from all of the tribes were simultaneously on the move over all parts of the Plains, with each party trying to anticipate the moves of the others in its area while it accomplished everything necessary to its own success.

Horse-raiding groups consisted of anything from four to twenty persons, depending upon the dream and estimates of the pipeholder. War parties ranged from fifteen upward to several hundred men, although even a party of one hundred was rare enough to be considered a mean force. Each group of raiders would include a few young men for training purposes, and on occasion a few women to do the cooking, although some wives went along intending to fight. Now and then dogs were taken along as pack animals. They were especially useful in the winter season.

The preferred time for departure was before sunup, so that when the rest of the village arose the adventurers would already be well on their way. Under average traveling conditions, a party on foot would make twenty-five miles per day on the way out, and might increase that pace on the return trip if they were unsuccessful.

A party on horseback would average fifty miles a day on the way toward the enemy, although the distance would vary in some ratio to the problems encountered after it entered enemy territory. Mounted war party members rode an average horse and led their prized war horses behind them, so as to keep these in prime condition for the demanding events ahead.

Some raiding trips were relatively short and were completed in two weeks, while others covered great distances, and the party might be gone from its home camp for several months. Blackfoot accounts tell of ancient war parties which left in the spring of one year and did not return till the summer or fall of the next. Sometimes the Blackfeet traveled all the way into Mexico, and returned with Spanish weapons and horse bits to prove it. Other Plains tribes say their war parties went as far west as the Pacific coast.

In starting out, a war party usually marched in the daytime, but sometimes traveled only at night from the beginning. Occasionally they would make an all-night march across a wide prairie where they might be seen if they traveled during the day. When parties traveled on foot, the experienced men carried their weapons while the boys in training bore the moccasins, ropes, food, and other equipment. The pipeholder had but little physical labor to perform. His mind was occupied with planning the movements of his party, and he was treated with the greatest respect. The others mended his moccasins, cared for his horses, and gave him the best of the food they carried or prepared.

All along the way the leader would seek to invoke dreams in an attempt to determine where his group would meet the enemy, how far away the foe was, and the size of his party or camp. On the night they reached the borderline area, all would smoke the sacred pipe and meditate upon the contents of the pipeholder's bundle. At this time the leader would pray for specific successes, and the others might make those impressive vows which would lead to their participation in Sun Dances. The men might also make sacrifices of favored possessions or of small slices of flesh, and deposit these on or before the bundle. At the border they also took fresh game, and packed the surplus meat in bags, so that fewer noises would be required later when they were in more dangerous places. They did their best to preserve their pemmican and dried meat for the direst emergencies.

On foot or horseback the war party traveled single file, with the war leader always in front. The experienced warriors came next, and the youngest men last. When the leader stopped, everyone else did the same. His commands were passed by word or hand signals back from one to the other. If ambushed, they went in all directions, with every man for himself. In enemy territory they remained as close together as wisdom and training dictated.

Shortly after leaving his village, the pipeowner would select at least two experienced young men to serve as scouts. Many of the warriors carried along wolfskins to be used as disguises for this service, and the Crows say that sometimes they daubed themselves with mud to look like wolves. Often, two advance scouts were sent ahead and to either side, and a third one acted as a rear guard.

The advance scouts often traveled by night so as to be at an advantageous lookout point when morning came. Having obtained their information by watching for all of the natural and animal signs, they then met the main body at a prearranged point and reported their findings. Every tribe had its own interesting ritual for this, and each was designed to produce an accurate story. Some kicked a waiting pile of buffalo chips. The main group of a Blackfoot raiding party prepared a pile of sticks for their scouts to kick over. Then the party members scrambled for the sticks, believing each stick recovered represented a horse they would take. A Kiowa scout coming in to report had a straw thrust through his hair "in a traditional manner" by the pipeholder, and as he removed it he told his story. It is said that an arrogant Kiowa leader sometimes pinched a scout hard to make certain he was telling the truth.

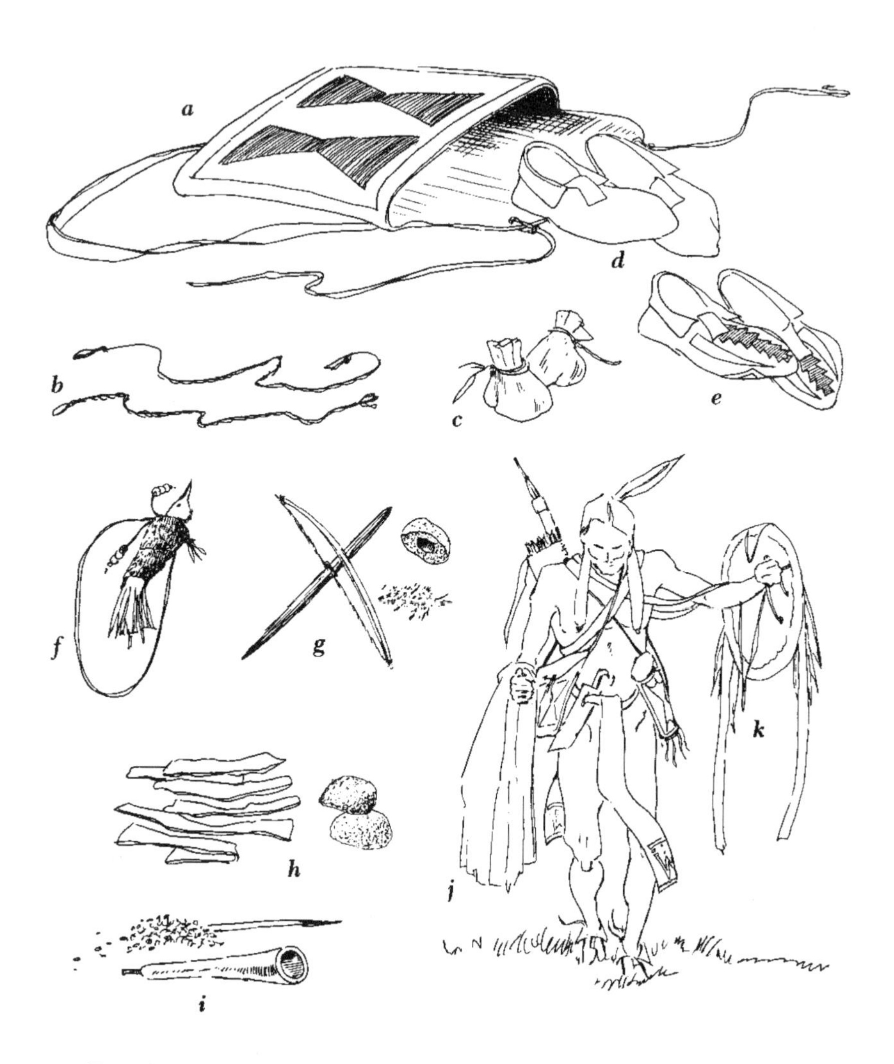

Typical gear carried by war and raiding parties. *a,* a rawhide carrying case or two, and clothing as required. *b,* extra bowstrings, carried in the quiver. *c,* war paint bags and shell for mixing. *d.* extra moccasins, sometimes carried in the covered shield. *e,* enemy moccasins to deceive their pursuers. *f,* personal medicine items, and the special war medicine. *g,* fire-making equipment, the old bow type or flint and steel. *h,* jerky and pemmican. *i,* pipe, tamper, and tobacco. *j,* a robe or blanket, sometimes rolled and strapped across the back infantry style. *k,* a shield if riding, but not always carried when on foot. A miniature shield or just the cover might be taken instead.

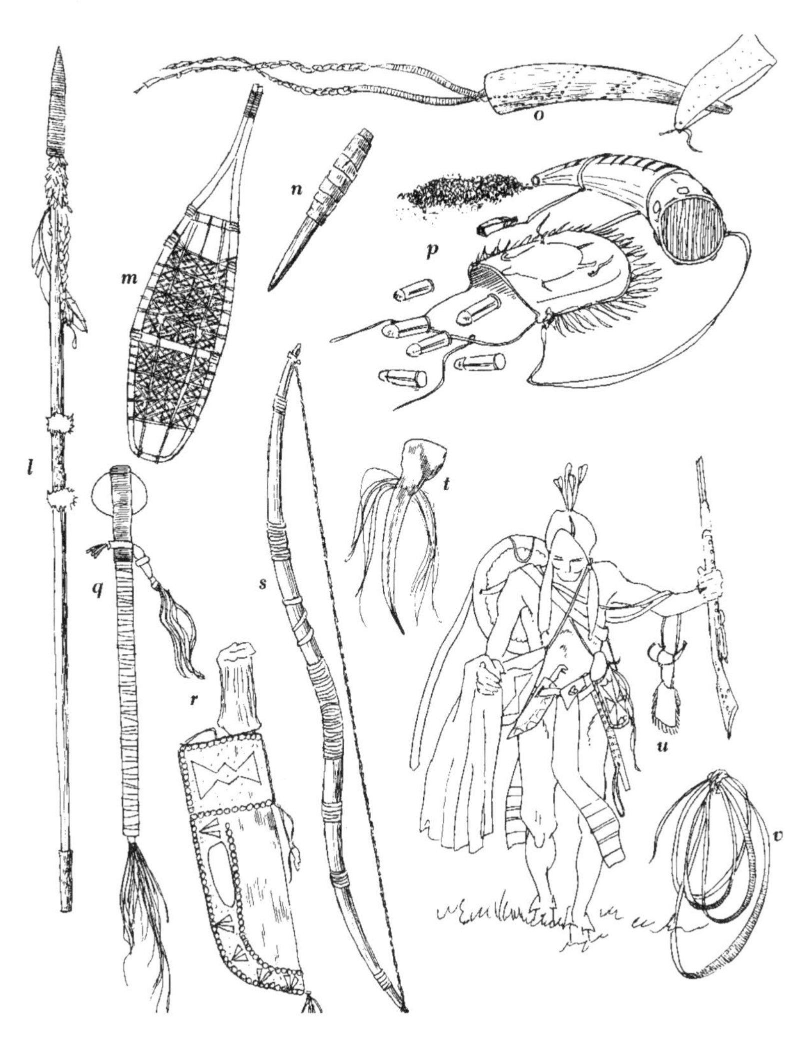

Typical gear continued. *l,* lances, a standard weapon for mounted warfare, and certainly not unknown to foot parties either, at least in short, lightweight versions. *m,* snowshoes for rough going in winter. *n,* a glue stick, carried in the quiver. *o,* a quirt. *p,* when guns were taken, the added equipment consisted of a powder horn or flask, and a patch bag for bullets or patches and round balls (see also u). *q,* clubs and/or tomahawks. *r,* a knife, usually a good-sized multipurpose one for skinning or battle. *s,* a bow, and perhaps an extra one for a war party, and about twenty arrows. *t,* a small supply of sinew and an awl. *u,* patch bag on leather straps. *v,* a rope to make a war bridle for stolen horses.

As a general rule the scouts and the war party traveled in ravines and coulees, so as to avoid being seen. In large war parties, the leader would often appoint one or more assistants to help lead the party, and these were identified by long, crooked staffs, which were made in the field of green saplings wrapped with fur or cloth.

Few fires were made in enemy country, and the men were careful about their foot tracks. If possible, camps were made in brushy or wooded areas. A typical one-night shelter was made of willow or cottonwood branches bent over after the nature of the sweat lodge. The branches were covered with brush, leaves, and blankets. The Blackfeet, and some of the other northern tribes, made a unique war lodge shelter of trees stacked in a tipi shape and covered with bark and leaves. Both field shelter types were designed to hide the campers and to diffuse the smoke from their fires. The war lodge closest to an enemy village became a base camp, though, and was believed to be an effective fort in case of attack. It was also the storage place for supplies to be used on the way home. Some accounts speak of rock shelters being prepared for the night. They also made excellent defense breastworks.

To cross rivers, the Mandans and the Hidatsas made a wood-frame, hide covered "bull boat." The Kiowas made a pontoon by wrapping deerskins around a pile of brush and bent willow branches. They even used this makeshift boat to ferry wounded men. The warrior was tied on the bundle and towed across by a swimmer—usually the pipeholder, since he gained prestige according to the number of men returning home with him.

The Crows lashed three sticks together to form a triangle, or four to make a rectangle, then spread a hide across them and tied it to the frame

Warrior loading muzzle loader by spitting balls into barrel while riding full tilt. Some authorities have questioned this as a common loading technique, but it was illustrated by F. Remington and by others.

edges to make a raft. A rock was placed in the center as a ballast. To cross deep, swift water they lashed three poles in a triangle and tied other poles across them to make a larger raft. Their guns and spears were then tied on top of the triangle in a tripod form, and the rest of their equipment was hung on this makeshift rack.

An alternate Crow method was to pile up several robes and to run a string around them to form a bundle. A rock ballast and articles to be kept dry were put in the middle. Among the Crows, the towing was done by the horses, or by men holding the towline of the rafts in their teeth.

The Shoshones piled bundles of bulrushes up and lashed them together till they made boats large enough to hold baggage weighing from six to eight hundred pounds.

Some warriors say they shot their arrows across a stream to keep them from getting wet. Swimmers usually crossed on the downstream side of their horses, with one arm hanging over their necks. An alternate method was to hold onto the horse's tail and let the horse pull them.

Some interesting side details of some of the Plains journeys are as follows:

A Kiowa war party, being caught in a place where water was scarce, licked the moisture seeping from some of the rocks in a cave. To climb down from a cliff, they tied their bows to their waists with the bowstrings, so that both hands would be free. Another time they used their bows as poles to help one another up the sides of steep places.

Crows riding down steep hills clung to the manes of their horses, so that even when they slid off they could boost themselves back on. Their water bags were made of buffalo stomachs closed by a drawstring.

Warriors in enemy territory dressing and painting on morning of battle.

Sioux party members always moved on the down side of the wind from animals or enemies. They said that the smell of fire or tobacco, or the sound of a snorting horse, were sure signs of danger. On horse-stealing trips, they rarely attacked a war party, but rather went around them so as to accomplish their primary purpose. One war leader states that he wore enemy clothing so that he would smell like them, and painted and fixed his hair in their manner—although he always wore his medicine underneath all of this!

When a small horse-raiding party had moved some distance into enemy country and came upon fresh tracks that clearly indicated the foe was nearby, the scouts began to look for a village to raid. Once one was discovered, a next-to-last camp was made ten or so miles away from the village, and the next day was spent in preparing for the raid.

Attention was given to weapons and other gear, to painting for battle, and to final prayers and supplications. Finally, the Native Americans' personal medicines were securely fixed in place. All food and surplus equipment, plus horses if they were riding, were left at the camp in the care of the first-timers, and that night the experienced warriors stripped for action and moved, under cover of darkness, to within sight of the village. This was the real moment of tenseness and excitement.

Ordinarily the pipeholder would scout the area, sometimes even sneaking into the village if a dance was going on. He might also do this if the village was very quiet, and in either case would return to advise the group as to how to proceed.

Some of them always went for the horses picketed at the tipis, since these were the greatest prizes, but while they did this the others cut away a part of the main herd in the pasture area. Depending upon the

Mounted war party.

situation they would get a few animals or a great many; perhaps sixty or more. If no suspicions were aroused they might even lead the first horses off a short distance, hobble them, and return for additional ones. The greater the risk, the better they liked it, and except at the time of the full moon, Plains sentries for some peculiar reason were often notoriously absent—as if to egg them on.

The raiders carried short ropes with them, and led some of the horses away with war bridles made from their ropes. Once they were a safe distance away from the village, they mounted the best horses and herded the others to their base camp. Here they would hastily pick up their gear, the young men, and be off for a ride that lasted at least two nights and a day before they slept. Pursuit by morning at the latest was inevitable, and they wanted to put as much distance as possible between themselves and the enemy. With so many horses, hiding the trail was almost impossible, and an advantageous head start was their only hope. More than one party was overtaken and badly mauled, and knowing this, they had little rest until the border of their own country was crossed.

The situation with a large war party was somewhat different than with that of a raiding group. A small war party would proceed with the same stealth as the horse-raiding group, but secrecy was out of the question for a large body of warriors. They knew they would be discovered shortly after—or perhaps even before—the enemy country was invaded, yet they took special courage in their medicines and strength. They moved, in any case, against enemy bands, which meant that they would face a force of equal or lesser number than their own. And nine times out of ten that force was on its way to meet them some distance from its village. Ambush was always preferred to an open encounter, and each body, as it approached, would be seeking just such a place and opportunity. Often defensive positions were taken in grass, bush, trees, or a washout. On many occasions rock breastworks were built in preparation for a pitched battle.

Hopefully, the invading body would have time to change into its full war regalia before the forces were enjoined. The Cheyenne say that most of their warriors preferred to dress—to impress the enemy, to take full advantage of their medicines, and to be ready to meet the One-Above in proper attire. Some, though, stripped for action. Those who did painted their bodies extensively, and were certain that their medicine preparations would save them from harm. The Cheyenne warriors had a special way of putting on their warbonnets and feathers, singing appropriate songs and raising the bonnets four times toward the sun, the fourth time putting them on while experienced instructors lectured them as to how to go into the fight.

Upon meeting the enemy in the open, and where all hope of surprise or advantage was gone, the leaders of both sides usually rode out to taunt their opponents, while the main bodies formed long lines

Sioux warrior praying for success in battle. Adapted from famous statue by Cyrus Dallin, 1913, Boston Museum. Battle gear added.

behind them. Sometimes the leader's main task was only to hold his young men back and in line. The taunting might go on for hours before mass action began. Once it did, there would first be firing from a distance, and then a mighty clash, with most battle plans forgotten and every man for himself. Each rode in singing his sacred war song, living his medicine to the fullest, and yelling at the top of his lungs to build up his courage.

The Cheyenne say that in a large battle the din was incredible. Horses ran into each other, and some fell and rolled. Clubs, hatchets, and lances were swung in every direction as everyone sought a coup, and the dust was so thick one could hardly see. One of their warriors scalped a member of his own tribe at the exhortation of others before any of them realized who the man was. A Crow, in pulling his gun from its case, accidentally shot his own horse!

Many said they lost all track of time and feeling; that when on foot "their feet hardly touched the ground." Most admitted they were exceedingly afraid, but went in anyway! After all, they had been taught that it was better to die young on the battlefield than to grow old and immobile in the tipi. As a rule, a fighting unit limited itself to a maximum of four passes in one place. After that it shifted its position or abandoned the battle. They did not circle very often, but made a fierce rush at the target, frequently jumping from their horses to fight on foot. Heroes par excellence were made by the rescuing of a fallen comrade, and the leaders in particular made every effort to bring all of their men home.

In relating their stories of battles, warriors did not hide the fact that they were subject to sudden and apparently causeless panics, while at

Blackfoot buffalo and war horses picketed at tipis.

other times they displayed unbelievable valor. Surely their opinions regarding the effectiveness of their medicines had much to do with this, and they were also omen-conscious. If friends began to fall in unexpected numbers, they took it as a clear sign from above to quit and get away, even though they knew that panic reduced their strength and made them easier prey to pursuing tribesmen. After all, they had done the same pursuing themselves. Yet they ran, because their medicine helpers had misfired somehow, or else they had misread their signs, and to stay would be to invite a worse tragedy still.

Generally speaking, losses in even a prolonged engagement involving hundreds of men would be fairly light, with a few being killed and a few more wounded. Everyone knew there would be another day to fight again, and they preserved themselves for it. The Comanches, who were a very large tribe in comparison to others in their area, were experts at this device. They overwhelmed small groups and literally cut them to bits. Yet if a single Comanche fell, they often ran—even when the numerical odds were still heavily in their favor.

The northern tribes were not so quick to do this, but they took any losses as a bad sign, and were glad to find an excuse to call it a day. All experts agree, however, that a badly wounded warrior became an absolute and totally reckless terror. One warrior was seen to fight like a tiger, and then to walk off with two bullets through his body close to his spine, the only effect of which was to cause him to change his gait from a run to a dignified walk.

Wounded men were transported home on a rough travois arrangement. The dead were retrieved if possible, but were often buried on the field in shallow graves or under rocks, the others leaving whatever gifts

a, Wolfskin for war party scout. *b*, wolfskin as collar prepared to be worn by Omaha warrior. *c*, wolfskin worn over shoulders by warrior.

they could to aid them in their journey to the Faraway Land. At home they would be mourned, but eminently respected. The Blackfoot parties had a unique custom of covering their battlefield dead with the bodies of their enemies. This was said to pay for those who were lost.

If an Assiniboine warrior was wounded, the person who rescued him counted it as a war deed. If a warrior brought back the dead and unscalped body of a comrade at the risk of his own life, that counted too. One who held the enemy off while the main body retreated was a major hero. If he made it back, he was elected to close the final dance in the victory celebration. The Crows mention instances where they covered fallen men with brush and returned later to retrieve their bodies.

Mutilation of fallen enemies was fairly common, with all tribes practicing it to some extent, the Blackfeet and Comanches being the worst.

Sometimes a body would be taken home for the women or children to count coup on, sometimes the limbs or fingers were removed, and it was fairly common to collect finger bones, which were made into necklaces to be worn at great festivals. A man who had one on when he fell in battle knew full well, however, what his own fate would be when the enemy found the bones.

Women and children captives were often adopted into the captor's tribe, soon to receive all of the rights and privileges of the camp's members. Yet when taken on a revenge raid they might as easily be killed as a warrior. Men were rarely captured. When they were caught, they were sometimes killed in cold blood, but more often were tortured before being put to death. Now and then a valiant captive would be kept for some time and then released, although his captivity was made exceedingly difficult and he was subjected to constant abuse.

Many a warrior who ran into serious trouble on a raid or war party, but escaped, experienced terrible problems in attempting to make his way home. Sometimes he suffered constantly for want of food or water.

One-night shelter of branches covered with blankets, type used by raiding party.

Northern Plains war lodge made of logs and bark, used as forts and storage houses by war parties.

Sometimes he nearly froze on the snow-covered prairie, or burned under a merciless sun. And when he finally made it back home, he might still be received as a failure who had shared in a tragic raid.

When the members of an Assiniboine war party arrived within sight of their home camp, they attracted the attention of the village by certain standard signs. If the party had been successful, a member trotted in a zigzag fashion. Then the people ran to greet them and took the scalps, horses, or other objects they had captured. A short dance followed, during which the objects were displayed. Everyone was happy. After that the owners often gave away everything they had taken to whomever they had in mind.

However, some warriors preferred to return to camp unannounced, after which they paraded their captured horses, and the entire camp held a victory dance. If the war party lost one or more members, they first attracted the people's attention, then they threw a robe, rolled into a ball-like shape, high in the air. The robe was thrown once for each member slain. A delegation was sent to meet the party and to obtain the names of the ones killed. The party was then escorted back to camp, and word was sent to the relatives of the slain—who immediately began their plaintive mourning customs.

Crow warriors always blackened their faces when they returned from a successful raid to indicate that any internal fires of revenge had burned out. They also used buffalo blood, mixed with charcoal, to paint symbols on robes wetted with clay to mark the coups which had been counted. Each count enabled them to decorate an area whose size was in proportion to the honor earned.

The Crow party approached their village and spent the night close to it. Early the next morning, they fired off their guns, gave characteristic yells, and thundered toward the camp, setting a grand victory celebration into motion which might last for several days.

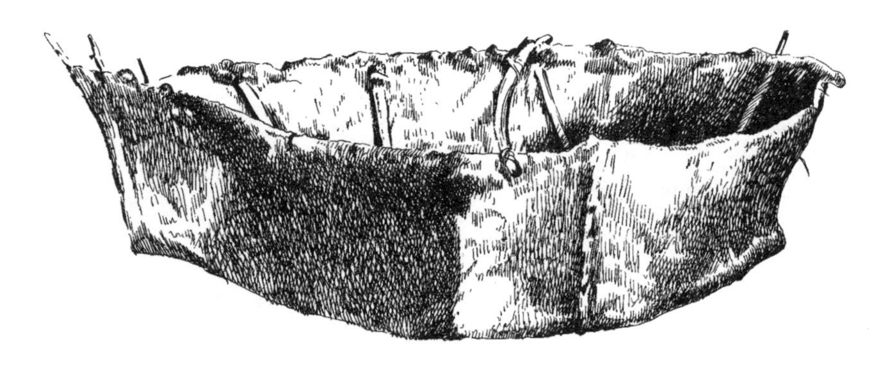

Mandan bull boat made of hide stretched over willow branches, about five feet in diameter.

The unsuccessful Crow parties did not enter the camp in an auspicious manner. A messenger was sent to a prominent place overlooking the camp to make a robe signal or to fire a gun. When everyone looked, he then lowered a blanket for each man killed, or threw it to one side. He then sat down and waited till the elders came to hear the story. Then the camp went into mourning while the party stayed in the hills for ten days. After this they gathered provisions, made preparations, and left on another raid, seeking success a second time, and a revenge death that could set their own bereaveds' minds at ease.

This was the way of life for the Native American warriors of all the Plains tribes. To them, the swift raids and the miniature wars were part of a very good life in which the days were enjoyed, not measured. As they put it, it was "the time when our hearts sang for joy."

Then the White settlers and army came, first decimating the unprepared Native Americans by infecting them with epidemics of cholera and smallpox and venereal diseases, and then finishing thousands more off by wars and by starvation through the elimination of the buffalo. Forcing them onto reservations where they were made totally dependent and placed in climates and areas which were unfamiliar to them completed the job of destroying a most commendable life-way.

"Then," said the Native Americans, "our hearts sank to the ground, and we did not have the strength to lift them up again." The singing and the dancing continued, but the songs and the dances became progressively meaningless and hollow. With the passing of the hunt and the warpath the rich ceremonies built around them lost their force. Nomads need to roam. Buffalo chants need buffalo. Pride finds its strength in usefulness. Crafts only flourish in happy days. Things did happen for the

Rafts used to carry goods across rivers and streams. *a, b,* and *c,* Crow method of making raft frames with skin tied across to transport small cargoes. *d,* warrior pulling raft by holding towline in mouth. *e,* triangular log raft for large cargoes.

Native Americans, yet they had no end purpose, no direction, no hope of arrival back at what they believed to be an excellent and worth-while life.

Warriors driving stolen horses.

Painted eagle bone war whistle with beaded pendant and eagle feather.